AN ANTHOLOGY OF INDIAN ENGLISH PROSE

AN ANTHOLOGY OF
INDIAN ENGLISH PROSE

Edited by

R.C. Prasad

J.P. Singh

MOTILAL BANARSIDASS

Delhi . Mumbai . Chennai . Kolkata

Bangalore . Varanasi . Patna

11th Reprint : 2018
First Edition : Delhi, 1988

ISBN : 978-81-208-0533-0

MOTILAL BANARSIDASS
41 U.A. Bungalow Road, Jawahar Nagar, Delhi 110 007
1 B, Jyoti Studio Compound, Kennedy Bridge, Nana Chowk, Mumbai 400 007
203 Royapettah High Road, Mylapore, Chennai 600 004
236, 9th Main III Block, Jayanagar, Bengaluru 560 011
8 Camac Street, Kolkata 700 017
Ashok Rajpath, Patna 800 004
Chowk, Varanasi 221 001

Printed in India
by RP Jain at NAB Printing Unit,
A-44, Naraina Industrial Area, Phase I, New Delhi–110028
and published by JP Jain for Motilal Banarsidass Publishers (P) Ltd,
41 U.A. Bungalow Road, Jawahar Nagar, Delhi-110007

PREFACE

Meant as this anthology of Indian English prose is for students studying for their Honours examination in English, it includes representative writings by some of the celebrated Indian writers —celebrated not only for their extra-literary attainments but also for their mastery of a variety of English which has come to be christened Indian English. We assume that there is not a reader, however ignorant, in any of the universities of India who is not familiar with these authors, some of whom are now an integral part of Indian political history.

These remarks, however, do not imply that there's no God's plenty here. Though Vivekananda, Aurobindo, Gandhi and Radhakrishnan may be grouped together—they are often grouped together—each of them has his own characteristic manner of using his medium and evinces qualities of his mind and personality so distinct from those of the others. This is applicable to the story-tellers as well. They recount stories but each in his own individual style, competent, muscled, vigorous, adroit and perspicuous. Their inclusion in this anthology has been guided by these inimitable qualities which the discerning reader will find only in the great story-tellers of the West—Maupassant, Chekhov, Henry James, Tolstoy, O'Henry, Somerset Maugham, Lawrence and Huxley, to name only a few out of myriads of master craftsmen of the art of story-telling.

Vivekananda's prose, like his personality, is thoroughly instinct with simplicity and evinces an intellect both spiritual and sublime. His endeavour to appeal to as many readers as possible determines the quality of his impassioned prose which is often as aphoristic as Seneca's or Lucan's. For prose of a complex kind full of cumulative passion and force, yet, subtly argumentative we shall have to turn to Sri Aurobindo, whose profound scholarship leaves its stamp upon every argument, whatever the subject matter. To Gandhi goes the credit for simplifying Indian English, for loading every idea with spirituality and for fusing thought with feeling. It is Gandhi's unified sensibility that can amalgamate disparate tendencies: politics and religion, art and science, etc. The very opening lines of his essay reveal the comprehensiveness of his interests and the mastery with which he brings to bear them on the topic about which he is writing. Gandhi's prose is the prose of conviction and confidence; it is the prose of one who can write with as much ease and facility as any English writer. Rajagopalachari puts forth new ideas in an appropriate garb, imposing though utterly simple. His "buts" and "ifs" exhibit an alertness for which Rajaji has been rightly famous. His prose is revelatory of an acute mind and an exceedingly sharp intellect and preoccupation, both moral and historical. His accent on the spiritual needs of school children provides the key to his mind and personality. As a prose writer, Radhakrishnan needs no introduction. Gifted with an analytical mind, subtle and scientific, he delights in providing pithy definitions and, before embarking upon a threadbare discussion of his theme, in taking the readers into full confidence. If Jawaharlal Nehru also achieves this purpose, the contributory factors are his utter humility and suavity coupled with his confessional tone and sensitivity. His is the prose of a self-conscious writer deeply involved in his experience and often sounding much too personal. The transparencies of his prose, however, and the limpidity of his ideas cast a spell upon the reader who would pounce upon his writings with uncontrollable avidity. Himself a man of inimitable culture, Nehru writes on culture with the insight of a seer and the acumen of a scholar.

Nirad C. Chaudhari has recently won notoriety for his diatribes against the intellectuals of the continent of Circe, but say what you will, he is a confident writer, well read, intelligent and mature, a writer whose prose has been hailed as near-Englishman's, vigorous and lively, an appropriate vehicle of his iconoclasm. The essay we have included in this anthology overflows with so many I's and reveals his personal concerns if not his idiosyncrasies. No reader will however miss the learning with which the arguments are buttressed and the prose enlivened.

Minoo Masani, whose political and economic commitments are well known, is often literary, allusive and, for the ordinary reader, abstruse. For the learned, he is consummate, adult and often justifiably journalistic.

The story tellers, all writers of repute, deal with diverse themes in diverse manners, each embodying his vision in a concrete, narrative form, and exploring an objective correlative for his experience. Since these stories are well known all attempts at their elucidation or evaluation are deemed futile, an exercise likely to affect their appreciation by the reader who must not be allowed to foster any prejudice nor forced to eulogise the authors.

R.C. Prasad
J.P. Singh

ACKNOWLEDGEMENTS

We are indebted to the following for permission to reproduce copyright material :—

Advaita Ashrama for 'The Secret of Work' from *Selections from Swami Vivekananda*; Sri Aurobindo Ashram for 'Internationalism' from *The Ideal of Human Unity* by Sri Aurobindo; the Navjivan Trust and Literary Executors of M.K. Gandhi for 'Indian Civilisation and Culture' from the book of the same name by M.K. Gandhi; All India Radio for 'Education for New India' by C. Rajagopalachari; the Publications Division, Government of India, for 'Science, Humanities and Religion' by S. Radhakrishnan and 'What is Culture ?' by Jawaharlal Nehru; Macmillan and Co. Ltd. for 'The Eternal Silence of These Infinite Crowds' by N. C. Chaudhari; Oxford University Press for 'No Man Is an Island' from *The Growing Human Family* by Minoo Masani; the Trustees of the Tagore Estate for 'The Babus of Nayanjore' from *Hungry Stones and Other Stories*; Dr Mulkraj Anand for 'The Brothers' from *Lajvanti and Other Stories*; Mr R.K. Narayan and Indian Thought Publications for 'An Astrologer's Day'; Oxford University Press for 'Companions' from *The Policeman and the Rose* by Raja Rao; Hind Pocket Books for 'Glory at Twilight' by Bhabani Bhattacharya from *Steel Hawk and Other Stories*; Kutub Popular Ltd for 'The Sparrows' from *Rice and Other Stories* by K.A. Abbas; Mr Khushwant Singh for 'Karma'; Miss Kamala Markandaya for 'The Flood' from *Nectar in a Sieve*; Siddhartha Publications for 'Circus Cat, Alley Cat' by Anita Desai from *Call It a Day*; Mr Arun Joshi for 'The Homecoming' first published in the Hindustan Times.

CONTENTS

ESSAYS

THE SECRET OF WORK

SWAMI VIVEKANANDA

The miseries of the world cannot be cured by physical help only. Until man's nature changes, his physical needs will always arise, and miseries will always be felt, and no amount of physical help will remove them completely. The only solution of the problem is to make mankind pure. Ignorance is the mother of evil and of all the misery we see. Let men have light, let them be pure and spiritually strong and educated; then alone will misery cease in the world. We may convert every house in the country into a charitable asylum; we may fill the land with hospitals, but human misery will continue until man's character changes.

We read in the *Bhagavad-Geeta* again and again that we must all work incessantly. We cannot do any work which will not do some good somewhere; there cannot also be any work which will not cause some harm somewhere. Every work must necessarily be a mixture of good and evil; yet we are commanded to work incessantly. Good and evil will both have their consequences. Good action will entail upon us good effect; bad action bad. But good and bad both forge fetters for the soul. The solution reached in the *Geeta* in regard to this cramping influence of work is, that if we do not attach ourselves to it, it will not hold our soul in bondage.

This is the one central idea in the *Geeta*; work incessantly, but be not attached to it. To use the simile of a lake for the mind, no ripple or wave that rises in it, dies out entirely, but it leaves a mark and there is a possibility of that wave coming out again. This mark, with the possibility of the wave reappearing, is what is called *Samskara*. Every work that we do, every movement of the body, every thought that we think, leaves such an impression on the mind-stuff, and even when the impressions are not obvious on the surface, they work in the subconscious region of the brain. What we are is determined every moment by the sum total of these impressions on the mind. What I am just at this moment, is the effect of the sum total of all the impressions of my past life. This is really what is meant by character; each man's character is determined by the sum total of these impressions. If good impressions prevail, the character becomes good; if bad, it becomes bad. If a man continuously hears bad words, thinks bad thoughts, does bad acts, his mind will be full of bad impressions; and they will influence his thought and work without his being conscious of the fact. These bad impressions will always be working, and their resultant must be evil, and the man will be a bad man : he cannot help it. The sum total of these impressions in him will create a strong motive power for doing bad acts. He will be like a machine in the hands of his impressions, and they will force him to do evil. Similarly, if a man thinks good thoughts and does good work, the sum total of their impressions will be good; and this, in a similar manner, will force him to do good even in spite of himself. When a man has done so much good work and thought so many good thoughts that there is an irresistible tendency in him to do good in spite of himself and even if he wishes to do evil, his mind, as the sum total of his tendencies, will not allow him to do so; these will hold him back. When such is the case, the man's good character is said to be established.

As the tortoise tucks its feet and head inside the shell and will not come out even though you may break the shell into pieces, even so the character of the man who has control over his motives and organs, is unchangeably established. He controls his own inner forces, and nothing can draw them out against his will. By this continuous reflex of good thoughts and good impressions moving over the surface of the mind, the tendency to do good becomes strong, and in consequence we are able to control the *Indriyas* (sense-organs, the nerve-centres). Thus alone is character formed, and only a man of character can get at truth. Such a man is safe for ever; he cannot do any evil. You may place him in any company, but there will be no danger for him. There is a still higher state than having this good tendency, and that is the desire for liberation. Liberation means full freedom—freedom from the bondage of good, as well as from the bondage of evil. A golden chain is as much a chain as an iron one. There is a thorn in my finger, and I use another to take the first one out, and when I have taken it out, I throw both of them aside. I have no necessity for keeping the second thorn, because it is a thorn after all. So bad tendencies are to be counteracted by good ones, and bad impressions on the mind should be removed by the fresh waves of good ones, until all that is evil almost disappears, or is subdued and held in control in a corner of the mind; but after that the good tendencies also have to be removed. Thus the 'attached' becomes the 'unattached'. Work, but let not the action or the thought produce a deep impression on your mind. Let the ripples come and go, let great actions proceed from the muscles and the brain, but let them not make any deep impression on the soul.

How can this be done? We see that the impression of every action to which we get attached remains. I may meet hundreds of persons during the day, and among them meet also one whom I love; but when I retire at night and try to think of all the faces I saw, only one face comes before the mind's eye—the face which I saw perhaps only for one minute and which I loved, all the others have vanished. Owing to my attachment to a particular person, his face caused a deeper impression on my mind than those of the others. But physically, the impressions have all been the same.

Therefore, be 'unattached', yet the brain-centres work; work incessantly, but let not the mind be affected. Work as if you were a stranger in this land, a sojourner; work incessantly, but do not bind yourselves; bondage is terrible. This world is not our habitation, it is only one of the many stages through which we are passing.

The gist of this teaching is that you should work like a master and not like a slave; work incessantly, but do not do slave's work. Do you not see how everybody works ? Nobody can be altogether at rest; ninety-nine per cent of men work like slaves, and the result is misery; it is all selfish work. But work with freedom, inspired by love ! There is no true love possible in the slave. If you buy a slave and tie him down in chains and make him work for you, he will work like a drudge, but there will be no love in him. So when we ourselves work for the things of the world as slaves, there can be no love in us, and work is not true work. This is true of work done for relatives and friends, and is true of work done for ourselves. Selfish work is slave's work; and here is a test. Every act of love brings happiness; there is no act of love which does not bring peace and blessedness in its train. Real existence, real knowledge, and real love are eternally connected with one another, the three in one; where one of them is, the others also must be; they are the three aspects of the One without a second—the Existence-Knowledge-Bliss.

Krishna says : 'Look at me, Arjuna ! If I stop from work for one moment, the whole universe will decay. I have nothing to gain from work : I am the one Lord, but why do I work ? Because I love the world.' God is unattached because He loves; real love makes us unattached.

To attain this unattachment is almost a life's work, but as soon as we have reached this point, we have attained the goal of love and become free; the bondage of nature falls from us, and we see nature as she is.

Do you ask anything of your children in return for what you have given them ? It is your duty to work for them, and there the matter ends. In whatever you do for a particular person, a city, or a state, assume the same attitude towards it as you have towards your children—expect nothing in return. If you can invariably take the position of a giver, in which everything given by you is a free offering to the world, without any thought of return, your work will bring you no attachment. Attachment comes only where we expect a return.

If working like slaves results in selfish attachment, working as masters of our own mind gives rise to the bliss of non-attachment. We often talk of right and justice, but we find that in this world right and justice are mere baby's talk. There are two things which guide the conduct of men : might and mercy. The exercise of might is invariably an act of selfishness. All men and women try to make the most of whatever power or advantage they have. Mercy is heavenly, to be good, we have all to be merciful. Even justice and right should stand on mercy. All thought of obtaining return for the work we do, hinders our spiritual progress; nay, in the end it brings misery. There is another way in which this idea of mercy and selfless charity can be put into practice; that is, by looking upon work as 'worship', Here we give up all the fruits of our work unto the Lord, and, worshipping Him thus, we have no right to expect anything from mankind for what we do. The Lord Himself works incessantly and is ever without attachment. Just as water cannot wet the lotus leaf, so work cannot bind the unselfish man by giving rise to attachment to results. The selfless and unattached man may live in the very heart of a crowded and sinful city, yet he will not be touched by sin.

INTERNATIONALISM

SRI AUROBINDO

The idea of humanity as a single race of beings with a common life and a common general interest is among the most characteristic and significant products of modern thought. It is an outcome of the European mind which proceeds characteristically from life-experience to the idea and, without going deeper, returns from the idea upon life in an attempt to change its outward forms and institutions, its order and system. In the European mentality it has taken the shape known currently as internationalism. Internationalism is the attempt of the human mind and life to grow out of the national idea and form and even in a way to destroy it in the interest of the larger synthesis of mankind. An idea proceeding on these lines needs always to attach itself to some actual force or developing power in the life of the times before it can exercise a practical effect. But usually it suffers by contact with the interest and prepossessions of its grosser ally, some lesser or greater diminution of itself or even a distortion, and in that form, no longer pure and absolute, enters on the first stage of practice.

The idea of internationalism was born of the thought of the eighteenth century and it took some kind of voice in the first idealistic stages of the French Revolution. But at that time, it was rather a vague intellectual sentiment than a clear idea seeing its way to practice; it found no strong force in life to help it to take visible body. What came out of the French Revolution and the struggle that grew around it, was a complete and self-conscious nationalism and not internationalism. During the nineteenth century we see the larger idea growing again in the minds of thinkers, sometimes in a modified form, sometimes in its own pure idealism, till allying itself with the growing forces of socialism and anarchism it took a clear body and a recognisable vital force. In its absolute form, it became the internationalism of the intellectuals, intolerant of nationalism as a narrow spirit of the past, contemptuous of patriotism as an irrational prejudice, a maleficent corporate egoism characteristic of narrow intellects and creative of arrogance, prejudice, hatred, oppression, division and strife between nation and nation, a gross survival of the past which the growth of reason was destined to destroy. It is founded on a view of things which looks at man in his manhood only and casts away all those physical and social accidents of birth, rank, class, colour, creed, nationality, which have been erected into so many walls and screens behind which man has hidden himself from his fellowman; he has turned them into sympathy-proof shelters and trenches from which he wages against him a war of defence and aggression, war of nations, war of continents, war of classes, war of colour with colour, creed with creed, culture with culture. All this barbarism the idea of the intellectual internationalist seeks to abolish by putting man face to face with man on the basis of their common human sympathy, aims, highest interests of the future. It is entirely futurist in its view; it turns away from the confused and darkened good of the past to the purer good of the future when man, at last beginning to become a truly intelligent and ethical being, will shake away from him all these sources of prejudice and passion and evil. Humanity will become one in idea and feeling, and life be consciously what it now is in spite of itself, one in its status on earth and its destiny.

The height and nobility of the idea is not to be questioned and certainly a mankind which sets its life upon this basis would make a better, purer, more peaceful and enlightened race than anything we can hope to have at present. But as the human being is now made, the pure idea, though always a great power, is also afflicted by a great weakness. It has an eventual capacity, once born, of taking hold of the rest of the human being and forcing him in the end to acknowledge its truth and make some kind of attempt to embody it; that is its strength. But also because man at present lives more in the outward than in the inward, is governed principally by his vital existence, sensations, feelings and customary mentality rather than by his higher thought-mind, and feels himself in these to be really alive, really to exist and be, while the world of ideas is to him something remote and abstract and, however powerful and interesting in its way, not a living thing, the pure idea seems, until it is embodied in life, something not quite real; in that abstractness and remoteness lies its weakness.

The sense of this abstractness imposes on the idea an undue haste to get itself recognised by life and embodied in a form. If it could have confidence in its strength and be content to grow, to insist, to impress itself till it got well into the spirit of man, it might conceivably become a real part of his soul-life, a permanent power in his psychology and might succeed in remoulding his whole life in its image. But it has inevitably a desire to get as soon as possible admitted into a form of life, for until then it does not feel itself strong and cannot quite be sure that it has vindicated its truth. It hurries into action before it has real knowledge of itself and thereby prepares its own disappointment, even when it seems to triumph and fulfil its object. For in order to succeed, it allies itself with powers and movements which are impelled by another aim than its own, but are glad enough to get its aid so that they may strengthen their own case and claim. Thus when it realises itself at last, it does it in a mixed, impure and ineffective form. Life accepts it as a partial habit, but not completely, not quite sincerely. That has been the history of every idea in succession and one reason at least why there is almost always something unreal, inconclusive and tormented about human progress.

There are many conditions and tendencies in human life at present which are favourable to the progress of the internationalist idea. The strongest of these favourable forces is the constant drawing closer of the knots of international life, the multiplication of points of contact and threads of communication and an increasing community in thought, in science and in knowledge. Science especially has been a great force in this direction; for science is a thing common to all men in its conclusions, open to all in its methods, available to all in its results; it is international in its very nature; there can be no such thing as a national science, but only the nations' contributions to the work and growth of science which are the indivisible inheritance of all humanity. Therefore it is easier for men of science or those strongly influenced by science to grow into the international spirit and all the world is now beginning to feel the scientific influence and to live in it. Science also created that closer contact of every part of the world with every other part, out of which some sort of international mind is growing. Even cosmopolitan habits of life are now not uncommon and there are a fair number of persons who are as much or more citizens of the world as citizens of their own nation. The growth of knowledge is interesting the peoples in each other's art, culture, religion, ideas and is breaking down at many points the prejudice, arrogance and exclusiveness of the old nationalistic sentiment. Religion, which ought to have led the way, but owing to its greater dependence on its external parts and its infra-rational rather than its spiritual impulses, has been as much, or even more, a sower of discord as a teacher of unity,—religion is beginning to realise, a little dimly and ineffectively as yet, that spirituality is after all its own chief business and true aim and that it is also the common element and the common bond of all religions. As these influences grow and come more and more consciously to co-operate with each other, it might be hoped that the necessary psychological modification will quietly, gradually, but still irresistibly and at last with an increasing force of rapidity, take place which can prepare a real and fundamental change in the life of humanity.

But this is at present a slow process, and meanwhile the internationalist idea, eager for effectuation, allied and almost identified itself with two increasingly powerful movements which have both assumed an international character, Socialism and Anarchism. Indeed, it is this alliance that most commonly went by the name of internationalism. But this socialistic and anarchistic internationalism was recently put to the test, the fiery test of the European war, and thus tried, it was found sadly wanting. In every country, the Socialist party shed its internationalist promise with the greatest ease and lightness, German socialism, the protagonist of the idea, massively leading the way in this formidable abjuration. It is true that a small minority in each country either remained heroically faithful to its principles or soon returned to them, and as the general weariness of the great international massacre grew, even the majority showed a sensible turn in the same direction; but this was rather the fruit of circumstance than of principle. Russian socialism, it may be said, has, at least in its extremer form, shown a stronger root of internationalistic feeling. But what it has actually attempted to accomplish is a development of Labour rule on the basis of a purified nationalism, non-aggressive except for revolutionary purposes and self-contained, and not on the larger international idea. In any case, the actual results of the Russian attempt show only up to the present a failure of the idea to acquire the vital strength and efficiency which would justify it to life; it is possible to use them much more as a telling argument against internationalism than as a justification of its truth or at least of its applicability in the present stage of human progress.

But what is the cause of this almost total bankruptcy of the international ideal under the strong test of life ? Partly it may be because the triumph of socialism is not necessarily bound up with the progress of internationalism. Socialism is really an attempt to complete the growth of the national community by making the individual do what he has never yet done, live for the community more than for himself. It is an outgrowth of the national, not of the international idea. No doubt, when the society of nations can and even must be formed; but this is a later possible or eventual result of Socialism, not its primary vital necessity. In the crises of life it is the primary vital necessity which tells, while the other and remoter element betrays itself to be a mere idea not yet ready for accomplishment; it can only become powerful when it also becomes either a vital or a psychological necessity. The real truth, the real cause of the failure is that internationalism is as yet, except with some exceptional men, merely an idea; it is not yet a thing near to our vital feelings or otherwise a part of our psychology. The normal socialist or syndicalist cannot escape from the general human feeling and in the test he too turns out, even though he were a professed *sans-patrie* in ordinary times, in his inner heart and being a nationalist. As a vital fact, moreover, these movements have been a revolt of Labour aided by a number of intellectuals against the established state of things, and they have only allied themselves with internationalism, because that too is an intellectual revolt and because its idea helps them in the battle. If Labour comes to power will it keep or shed its internationalistic tendencies? The experience of countries in which it is or has been at the head of affairs does not give an encouraging answer, and it may at least be said that, unless at that time the psychological change in humanity has gone much farther than it has now, Labour in power is likely to shed more of the internationalist feeling than it will succeed in keeping and to act very much from the old human motives.

No doubt, the European war itself was an explosion of all that was dangerous and evil in successful nationalism, and the resulting conflagration may well turn out to have been a purificatory process that has burned up many things that needed to die. It has already strengthened the international idea and forced it on governments and peoples. But we cannot rely too greatly on ideas and resolutions formed in a moment of abnormal crisis under the violent stress of exceptional circumstances. Some effect there may be in the end, some first recognition of juster principles in international dealings, some attempt at a better, more rational or at least a more convenient international order. But until the idea of humanity has grown not only upon the intelligence but in the sentiments, feelings, natural sympathies and mental habits of man, the progress made is likely to be more in external adjustments than in the vital matters, more in a use of the ideal for mixed and egoistic purposes than at once or soon in a large and sincere realisation of the ideal. Until man in his heart is ready a profound change of the world conditions cannot come; or it can only be brought about by force, physical force or else force of circumstances, and that leaves all the real work to be done. A frame may have then been made, but the soul will have still to grow into that mechanical body.

INDIAN CIVILIZATION AND CULTURE

M. K. Gandhi

I believe that the civilization India has evolved is not to be beaten in the world. Nothing can equal the seeds sown by our ancestors. Rome went, Greece shared the same fate, the might of the Pharaohs was broken, Japan has become Westernized; of China nothing can be said, but India is still, somehow or other, sound at the foundation. The people of Europe learn their lessons from the writings of the men of Greece or Rome which exist no longer in their former glory. In trying to learn from them, the Europeans imagine that they will avoid the mistakes of Greece and Rome. Such is their pitiable condition.

In the midst of all this, India remains immovable and that is her glory. It is a charge against India that her people are so uncivilized, ignorant and stolid, that it is not possible to induce them to adopt any changes. It is a charge really against our merit. What we have tested and found true on the anvil of experience, we dare not change. Many thrust their advice upon India, and she remains steady. This is her beauty, it is the sheet anchor of our hope.

Civilization is that mode of conduct which points out to man the path of duty. Performance of duty and observance of moraltiy are convertible terms. To observe morality is to attain mastery over our minds and our passions. So doing, we know ourselves. The Gujarati equivalent for civilization means "good conduct".

If this definition be correct, then India, as so many writers have shown, has nothing to learn from anybody else, and this is as it should be.

We notice that the mind is a restless bird, the more it gets the more it wants, and still remains unsatisfied. The more we indulge in our passions, the more unbridled they become. Our ancestors, therefore, set a limit to our indulgences. They saw that happiness was largely a mental condition.

A man is not necessarily happy because he is rich, or unhappy because he is poor. The rich are often seen to be unhappy, the poor to be happy. Millions will always remain poor. Observing all this, our ancestors dissuaded us from luxuries and pleasures. We have managed with the same kind of plough as existed thousands of years ago. We have retained the same kind of cottages that we had in former times and our indigenous education remains the same as before. We have had no system of life-corroding competition. Each followed his own occupation or trade and charged a regular wage. It was not that we did not know how to invent machinery, but our forefathers knew that, if we set our hearts after such things, we would become slaves and lose our moral fibre. They, therefore, after due deliberation decided that we should only do what we could with our hands and feet. They saw that our real happiness and health consisted in a proper use of our hands and feet.

They further reasoned that large cities were a snare and a useless encumbrance and that people would not be happy in them, that there would be gangs of thieves and robbers, prostitution and vice flourishing in them and that poor men would be robbed by rich men. They were, thorefore, satisfied with small villages.

They saw that kings and their swords were inferior to the sword of ethics, and they, therefore, held the sovereigns of the earth to be inferior to the Rishis and the Fakirs. A nation, with a constitution like this, is fitter to teach others than to learn from others. This nation had courts, lawyers and doctors, but they were all within bounds. Everybody knew that these professions were not particularly superior. Moreover, these Vakils and Vaids did not rob people, they were considered people's dependents, not their masters. Justice was tolerably fair. The ordinary rule was to avoid courts. There were no touts to lure people into them. This evil too was noticeable only in and around capitals. The common people lived independently and followed their agricultural occupation. They enjoyed true Home Rule.

The Indian civilization, as described by me, has been so described by its votaries. In no part of the world, and under no civilization, have all men attained perfection. The tendency of the Indian civilization is to elevate the moral being, that of the Western civilization is to propagate immorality. The latter is godless, the former is based on a belief in God. So understanding and so believing, it behoves every lover of India to cling to the old Indian civilization even as a child clings to the mother's breast.

I am no hater of the West. I am thankful to the West for many a thing I have learnt from Western literature. But I am thankful to modern civilization for teaching me that if I want India to rise to its fullest height, I must tell my countrymen frankly that, after years and years of experience of modern civilization, I have learnt one lesson from it and that is that we must shun it at all costs.

What is that modern civilization? It is the worship of the material, it is the worship of the brute in us—it is unadulterated materialism, and modern civilization is nothing if it does not think at every step of the triumph of material civilization.

It is perhaps unnecessary, if not useless, to weigh the merits of the two civilizations. It is likely that the West has evolved a civilization suited to its climate and surroundings, and similarly, we have a civilization suited to our conditions, and both are good in their own respective spheres.

The distinguishing characteristic of modern civilization is an indefinite multiplicity of human wants. The characteristic of ancient civilization is an imperative restriction upon, and a strict regulating of, these wants. The modern or Western insatiableness arises really from want of living faith in a future state and therefore also in Divinity. The restraint of ancient or Eastern civilization arises from a belief, often in spite of ourselves, in a future state and the existence of a Divine Power.

Some of the immediate and brilliant results of modern inventions are too maddening to resist. But I have no manner of doubt that the victory of man lies in that resistance. We are in danger of bartering away the permanent good for a momentary pleasure.

Just as in the West they have made wonderful discoveries in things material, similarly Hinduism has made still more marvellous discoveries in things of religion, of the spirit, of the soul.

But we have no eye for these great and fine discoveries. We are dazzled by the material progress that Western science has made. I am not enamoured of that progress. In fact, it almost seems as though God in his wisdom had prevented India from progressing along those lines, so that it might fulfil its special mission of resisting the onrush of materialism.

After all, there is something in Hinduism that has kept it alive up till now. It has witnessed the fall of Babylonian, Syrian, Persian and Egyptian civilizations. Cast a look around you. Where is Rome and where is Greece? Can you find today anywhere the Italy of Gibbon, or rather the Ancient Rome, for Rome was Italy?

Go to Greece. Where is the world-famous Attic civilization? Then coming to India, let one go through the most ancient records and then look around you and you would be constrained to say, "yes, I see here ancient India still living".

True, there were dungheaps, too, here and there, but there

are rich treasures buried under them. And the reason why it has survived is that the end which Hinduism set before it was not development along matetial but spiritual lines.

Our civilization, our culture, our Swaraj depend not upon multiplying our wants—self-indulgence, but upon restricting wants—self-denial.

European civilization is, no doubt, suited for the Europeans but it will mean ruin for India if we endeavour to copy it. This is not to say that we may not adopt and assimilate whatever may be good and capable of assimilation by us, as it does not also mean that even the Europeans will not have to part with whatever evil might have crept into it.

The incessant search for material comforts and their multiplication is such an evil and I make bold to say that the Europeans themselves will have to remodel their outlook, if they are not to perish under the weight of the comforts to which they are becoming slaves. It may be that my reading is wrong, but I know that for India to run after the Golden Fleece is to court certain death. Let us engrave on our hearts the motto of a Western philosopher: "Plain living and high thinking". Today it is certain that the millions cannot have high living and we the few, who profess to do the thinking for the masses, run the risk, in a vain search after high living, of missing high thinking.

Civilization, in the real sense of the term, consists not in the multiplication, but in the deliberate and voluntary restriction of wants. This alone increases and promotes contentment, real happiness and capacity for service.

A certain degree of physical harmony and comfort is necessary but above a certain level it becomes a hindrance instead of help. Therefore, the ideal of creating an unlimited number of wants and satisfying them seems to be a delusion and a snare. The satisfaction of one's physical needs, even the intellectual needs of one's narrow self, must meet at a certain point a dead stop, before it degenerates into physical and intellectual voluptuousness. A man must arrange his physical and cultural circumstances so that they do not hinder him in his service of humanity on which all his energies should be concentrated.

EDUCATION FOR NEW INDIA

C. Rajagopalachari

Freedom has assuredly given us a new status and new opportunities. But it also implies that we should discard selfishness, laziness and narrowness of outlook. Our freedom suggests toil and creation of new values for old ones. We should so discipline ourselves as to be able to discharge our new responsibilities satisfactorily. If there is any one thing that needs to be stressed more than any other in the new set-up, it is that we should put into action our full capacity, each one of us in productive effort —each one of us in his own sphere, however humble. Work, unceasing work, should now be our watch-word. Work is wealth, and service is happiness. Nothing else is. The greatest crime in India today is idleness. If we root out idleness, all our difficulties, including even conflicts, will gradually disappear. Whether as constable or high official of the State, whether as a businessman or industrialist, artisan or farmer or peasant, each one of us is discharging his obligation to the State and making a contribution to the welfare of the country. Honest work is the sheet-anchor to which we should cling if we want to be saved from danger or difficulty. It is the fundamental law of progress.

Next to honest work is the habit of respecting other people's feelings. It takes all sorts to make this world, and the highest virtue of every citizen is to try so to conduct himself that a mode of life may be evolved by which people of differing religious faiths, occupations and attainments who constitute our society, may live in peace and amity. The law of love is a practical code of life, as our dear departed leader so strenuously sought to teach us. My confirmed opinion is that in India there is in fact no communal hatred. Greed and fear of defeat in economic competition produce what is mistaken for communal ill-feeling. There is abundant and abiding respect for all kinds of creeds, faiths and ways of life, but selfishness and personal ambitions produce conditions of mind often mistaken for communal ill-will. It is not, therefore, a hopeless task to restore and maintain communal amity.

To manage the affairs of an independent state, trained leadership is necessary. You have had training in that direction in some measure, for University education is nothing but a training for leadership. Numberless citizens are denied this privilege, and you should therefore regard your good fortune as a precious debt. In your daily conduct, in whatever walk of life you may be and under all conditions, you should remember your obligation of leadership and an example to others how to think and speak and how to act, The physical defence of a State is the special responsibility of the members of the Forces. You are the moral and cultural army of India. Her progressive culture and contribution to world-civilization should be your concern. That the youth of today are the citizens of tomorrow is a trite saying. But in a land that has just attained political freedom the citizens have to shoulder new responsibilities in every field of national activity, and you, young graduates, should mark in that oft-repeated statement a vital significance that concerns you intimately.

I would suggest to educationists that less stress should be laid on examinations and more on opportunities for study and assimilation. The examination is the most bitter form of compulsion. It creates an incurable tendency towards superficiality and a paradoxical condition wherein a certain degree of equipment and dislike go together. It leaves in the successful candidate a distaste for further study, once the examination is over. If in any field the standard of attainment is better in foreign universities than in India, it is not due to stiffer examination or to superior talents. It is the result of greater voluntary exertion on the part of teachers and pupils born of their love of work, and better facilities for study and research, rather than of any stricter or better system of examinations and rejections. It is the outcome of a condition of things in which aptitude and love of knowledge rather than irrelevant ambitions and prospects of career and employment guide the students in their choice of studies.

There are two problems which cause great worry to our educationists, the problem of religious and moral instruction in a land of many faiths, and the problem arising out of a large variety of languages. Taking up the education of children, we see that they should be trained to love one another, to be kindly and helpful to all, to be tender to the lower animals, and observe and think aright. The task of teaching them how to read and write and to count and calculate is important, but it should not make us lose sight of the primary aim of moulding personality in the right way. For this it is necessary to call into aid culture, tradition and religion. But in our country we have, in the same school, to look after boys and girls born in different faiths and belonging to families that live diverse ways of life and follow forms of worship associated with different denominations of religion. It will not do to tread the easy path of evading the difficulty by attending solely to physical culture and intellectual education. We have to evolve a suitable technique and method for serving the spiritual needs of school children professing different faiths. We would thereby promote an atmosphere of mutual respect, a fuller understanding and helpful cooperation among the different communities in our society. Again, we must remain one people, and we have therefore to give basic training in our schools to speak and understand more languages than one and to appreciate and respect the different religions prevailing in India. It is not right for us in India to be dissuaded from this by considerations as to over-taxing the young mind. What is necessary must be done. And it is not in fact too great a burden.

As for the language, it is no good trying to impose a medium of instruction on young pupils, which is not their mother-tongue. In the past, parents preferred their children to undergo the disadvantages of the English medium because, as against the drawbacks of a foreign medium, the advantages in life of superficially Anglicised culturc were great. They deliberately allowed their children to learn the language through subjects rather than subjects through the language, because facility in the use of the English language helped one very largely and covered many defects. These advantages must now soon disappear and the drawbacks in using a foreign medium will be more and more obvious as we go on. Nothing is gained by depriving young boys and girls of the advantages of the mother-tongue or some language near to it. In regions where more than one language is spoken, I see no other way but one, namely, to form sections in the mixed schools according to language. For certain purposes they may sit together, so that the advantages of both mixing and separate attention may be retained. Provided we try to solve the problems with understanding and patience, the very difficulties which we first deplore, often prove in the end to be of the greatest value for progress. What was pain and trouble becomes a source of enlightenment and joy.

Restraint in behaviour and consideration for the feelings of others are what distinguish a man of culture. Be patient and kind always. Do not give way to jealousy or the desire to boast. Be not rude. Do not always insist on having your own way. Do not allow yourself to be irritated or be resentful. Do not rejoice at wrong. Rejoice in the right. Try to bear misfortunes bravely. Show trust in others and have faith that love will prevail. This is what Paul said. This is what Gandhi said.

SCIENCE, HUMANITIES AND RELIGION

S. RADHAKRISHNAN

A University is essentially a community of students and teachers. The two have to work together for the one single purpose of advancing knowledge and disseminating it. If they are at any time distracted from this straight path of pursuing truth for its own sake and get led away, there will be a jeopardy to the community of the university. I have no doubt, here the teachers and students are working together.

Your Vice-Chancellor asked us to forget all the incidents of last year and if you are noble, you will not only forget but forbear and adopt and attitude of forgiveness towards all the incidents of the past.

It is easy to win freedom but very difficult to preserve it. We have now 480 million people in our country and we can be said to be really free if we are able to provide them with food, clothing, shelter and employment.

How far we are from that goal is evident to every one of you and it is the distance we have to travel that has to be taken into account. Each one of you has a responsibility. We come to the universities to be equipped with the knowledge and the skill by which we will be able to help the building of our country. Are we doing it? Are the universities providing the right material for the nation-building operation? Are they giving them the knowledge and the skill which are essential for any kind of process? You come here to study sciences, to study humanities, to study theology also, which is not an unimportant science. Science itself is necessary because the wonders of science have transformed this world. For transport we had the horse, the bicycle, the automobile, etc. Now, the other day, I heard that a rocket-ship can take us from one place to another in a space of 25 minutes. These are all great achievements which we have to participate in. Every one of us must feel that as the achievements of science are spreading, we have also some contribution to make so far as these achievements are concerned. It is wrong to think as once upon a time Blake said, 'The tree of life is sustained by art, the tree of death by science'. It is a misleading conception; science may be abused but that is not the fault of science; that is the fault of man. It is, therefore, essential for us to provide our students with the best that is possible in sciences and technology. It is these things that help us to provide the necessities for our people.

Humanities again are important because they tell us about our own nature; how we have to grow from day to day. What the impulses are, what the ideals and aspirations are, these are the things that we have to learn from the humanities. But whether it is sciences or humanities, whether they are natural sciences or social sciences, they touch only the periphery of the reality, they touch only the outside, the expression, the multiplicity of manifestations. But what the central being is, you have to learn also if a student is to consider himself to be really educated. Mere sciences, natural or social, are not enough. You have to exercise yourself, what is called some kind of solitary reflectiou or meditation by which you reach the centre of your being from which all other things emanate. What is it that science does? It evaluates. It is an adventure of mind, an imaginative adventure of mind. What is responsible for it? The living spirit of man. It is never content with ignorance, it always tries to break down ignorance and provide some kind of knowledge.

What do humanities do? They also use the same powers of human mind but on other data, on human data, of relationships between man and man. But the living spirit itself is, not directly contacted by you, either by sciences or by humanities. Directly, they do not reveal to you what the living spirit of man is, of which sciences and humanities are both expressions. For that, arts, literature and religion are essential. Religion, not in the sense of dogmatic, sectarian religion, which makes us hate one another but the true spirit of religion, inward awareness and outward compassion. Religion which your Quranic prayer just uttered tells us. It is that religion of recognising humbly, respectfully, thar there is a superior being, a higher Reality of which we are all the offshoots. It is that kind of religion. Masnavi in his great book says: 'The moon is in the sky, not in this stream; in this stream what you find is reflection'. But the Reality is raised above the phenomenal world; it is something which you cannot grasp by merely losing yourself in the manifestations of the world. You have to look above and how you look does not depend upon this dictator or that prophet; it depends on the nature of man. It is the Sufi poet who said, that there are as many ways to God as there are human hearts. There is no one royal road to salvation. There is no one stereotyped method by which we can attain the Reality. We have to give absolute elasticity, we have to be hospitable to every kind of direction. Your great prophet, Mohammad, has said that God has not refused messenger to any community. Every community has its own messenger and the Constitution of our country embodies this fundamental principle when it says we must have the liberty to profess, propagate and practise whatever religion we want.

I hope that in this University these three things, sciences, humanities and religion, are worked together as parts of one whole. Human knowledge cannot be divided against itself. Everything that you do is both secular and sacred. Everything that you do is done with the background of eternity. You cannot do a thing unless you have that sense that we are all humble creatures in this world, asked to carry out our particular avocations or activities. The world is moving. It is 10,000 years ago that civilization started and since then we have marched forward from one stage to another. The process in which we are now engaged is the process of attaining unification of the whole world. Whatever studies we have, whatever learning we possess, whatever skill we acquire, we must take a pledge that we will use them for the betterment of humanity, for the betterment of the human race, for bringing the goal of one world nearer. It is that kind of pledge that every graduate should take.

I am glad that I have become today one of you and you have got your degrees and some of you have attained distinction. We are all working together for one common purpose. That common purpose must endow every students. Never think harshly of anybody; be may be estranged from you, he may be betrayed, he may be corrupted, he may be deformed; whatever it might be, he is a brother man after all. You must remember that he is a man who has also got the chances of growing and of developing. That is what we are all aiming at in this world.

It is my earnest hope that this university may attain to greater eminence in intellectual achievement and moral leadership and every one of you will feel pround to be a graduate of Aligarh on account of the glory that it has attained. It is you people who have to contribute to the achievement of that glory. It is my greatest ambition, earnest hope, that this University may attain a place in the international world as one of the great universities of the world, by the work you do, not merely by shouting slogans. By shouting slogans we cannot achieve anything, but by the honest work which we do, in an honest and noble spirit in a dedicated way. After all, whether it is an achievement in science or technology or humanities or religion, what is responsible for that is the great spirit in you. If you become alienated from it, you will suffer from neurosis, you will suffer from every kind of mental disability. Why are there so many mental cases today? Because they have been alienated from the centre of their being, that is the centre from which everything emanates.

If you remember that centre, you will never be alienated. You will be free from anxiety even in the most breathtaking situations; whatever may happen, you will retain your calm and composure. If only you are sure of the bedrock within you, if you are able to delve into it, if you are able to take note of it, then you will feel that the whole humanity is one kindred and there is one God. Nothing greater has been uttered in this world. 'There is one God and one family on earth'.

WHAT IS CULTURE?

JAWAHARLAL NEHRU

I have come here with pleasure because I have always looked forward to furthering the cause of India's cultural association, not only with the neighbouring countries to the East and West but with the wider world outside. It is not a question of merely wanting such cultural association or considering it good; it is rather a question of the necessity of the situation which is bound to worsen if nothing is done to prevent. I earnestly hope that the formation of the India Council of Cultural Relations will lead to a better understanding between our people and the peoples of other countries.

There is a great deal of confusion in my mind and I shall state quite frankly what it is. All kinds af basic questions crop up from what is going on in the world around us. Nations, individuals and groups talk of understanding one another, and it seems an obvious thing that people should try to understand one another and to learn from one another. Yet, when I look through the pages of history or study current events, I sometimes find that people who know one another most, quarrel most. Countries, which are next door to one another in Europe or in Asia, somehow seem to rub one another the wrong way, though they know one another very thoroughly. Thus, knowledge, by itself does not lead to greater co-operation or friendship. This is not a new thing. Even the long pages of history show that. Has there been something wrong in individual nations or in the approach to this question? Or is it something else that has not worked as it should have done? When we talk of cultural relations, the question that immediately arises in my mind is—What exactly is the 'culture' that people talk so much about? When I was younger in years, I remember reading about German 'Kultur' and of the attempts of the German people to spread it by conquest and other means. There was a big war to spread it by conquest and other means. There was a big war to spread this 'Kultur' and to resist it. Every country and every individual seem to have their peculiar idea of culture. When there is talk about cultural relations—although it is very good in theory—What actually happens is that those peculiar ideas come into conflict and instead of leading to friendship they lead to more estrangement. It is a basic question—what is culture? And I am certainly not competent to give you a definition of it because I have not found one.

One can see each nation and each separate civilization developing its own culture that had its roots in generations hundreds and thousands of years ago. One sees these nations being intimately moulded by the impulse that initially starts a civilization going on its long path. That conception is affected by other conceptions and one sees action and interact on between these varying conceptions. There is, I suppose, no culture in the world which is absolutely pristine, pure and unaffected by any other culture. It simply cannot be, just as nobody can say that he belongs one hundred per cent to a particular racial type, because in the course of hundreds and thousands of years unmistakable changes and mixtures have occurred.

If that kind of thing goes on peacefully, there is no harm in it. But it often leads to conflicts. It sometimes leads a group to fear that their culture is being overwhelmed by what they consider to be an outside or alien influence. Then they draw themselves into a shell which isolates them and prevents their thoughts and ideas going out. That is an unhealthy situation, because in any matter and much more so in what might be called a cultural matter, stagnation is the worst possible thing.

Culture, if it has any value, must have a certain depth. It must also have a certain dynamic character. After all, culture depends on a vast number of factors. If we leave out what might be called the basic mould that was given to it in the early stages of a nation's or a people's growth it is affected by geography, by climate and by all kinds of other factors. The culture of Arabia is intimately governed by the geography and the deserts of Arabia because it grew up there. Obviously, the culture of India in the old days was affected greatly, as we see in our own literature, by the Himalayas, the forests and the great rivers of India among other things. It was natural growth from the soil. Of the various domains of culture, like architecture, music and literature any two may mix together, as they often did and produce a happy combination. But where there is an attempt to improve something or the other which does not naturally grow and mould itself without uprooting itself, conflict inevitably arises. Then also comes something which to my mind is basically opposed to all ideas of culture. And that is the isolation of the mind and the deliberate shutting up of the mind to other influences. My own view of India's history is that we can almost measure the growth and the advance of India and the decline of India by relating them to periods when India had her mind open to the outside world and when she wanted to close it up. The more she closed it up, the more state she became. Life, whether of the individual group, nation or society, is essentially a dynamic, chaging, growing thing. Whatever stops that dynamic growth also injures it and undermines it.

We have had great religions and they have had an enormous effect on humanity. Yet, if I may say so with all respect and without meaning any ill to any person, those very religions, in the measure that they made the mind of man static, dogmatic and bigoted, have had, to my mind, an evil-effect. The things they said may be good but when it is claimed that the last word has been said, society becomes static.

The individual human being or race or nation must necessarily have a certain depth and certain roots somewhere. They do not count for much unless they have roots in the past, which past is after all the accumulation of generations of experience and some type of wisdom. It is essential that you have that. Otherwise you become just palecopies of something which has no real meaning to you as an individual or as a group. On the other hand one cannot live in roots alone. Even roots wither unless they come out in the sun and the free air. Only then can the roots give you sustenance. Only then can there be branching out and a flowering. How, then, are you to balance these two essential factors? It is very difficult, because some people think a great deal about the flowers and the leaves on the branches, forgetting that they only flourish because there is a stout root to sustain them. Others think so much of the roots that no flowers or leaves or branches are left; there is only a thick stem somewhere. So, the question is how one is to achieve a balance.

Does culture mean some inner growth in the man? Of course, it must. Does it mean the way he behaves to others? Certainly it must. Does it mean the capacity to understand the other person? I suppose so. Does it mean the capacity to make yourself understood by the other person? I suppose so. It means all that. A person who cannot understand another's view point is to that extent limited in mind and culture, because nobody, perhaps, barring some very extraordinary human beings, can presume to have the fullest knowledge and wisdom. The other party or the other group may also have some inkling of knowledge or wisdom or truth and if we shut our minds to that then we not only deprive ourselves of it but we cultivate an attitude of mind which, I would say, is opposed to that of a cultured man. The cultured mind, rooted in itself, should have its windows and doors open. It should have the capacity to understand the other's view-point fully even though it cannot always agree with it. The question of agreement or disagreement only arises when you understand a thing. Otherwise, it is blind negation which is not a cultured approach to any question.

Nationalism, of course, is a curious phenomenon which at a certain stage in a country's history gives life, growth, strength and unity but, at the same time, it has a tendency to limit one, because one thinks of one's country as something different from the rest of the world. Their perspective changes and one is continuously thinking of one's own struggles and virtues and failings to the exclusion of other thoughts. The result is that the same nationalism, which is the symbol of growth for a people, becomes a symbol of the cessation of that growth in the mind. Nationalism when it becomes successful, sometimes goes on spreading in an aggressive way and becomes a danger internationally. Whatever line of thought you follow, you arrive at the conclusion that some kind of balance must be found. Otherwise something that was good can turn into evil. Culture, which is essentially good becomes not only static but aggressive and something that breeds conflict and hatred when looked at from a wrong point of view. How are you to find a balance, I do not know. Apart from the political and economic problems of the age, perhaps that is the greatest problem today because behind it there is a tremendous search for something which it cannot find. We turn to economic theories because they have an undoubted importance. It is folly to talk of culture or even of God when human beings starve and die. Before one can talk about anything else one must provide the normal essentials of life to human beings. That is where economics comes in. Human beings today are not in the mood to tolerate this suffering and starvation and inequality when they see that the burden is not equally shared. Others profit while they only bear the burden.

We have inevitably to deal with these problems in economic and other ways but we do not think that behind it all there is a tremendous psychological problem in the minds of the people.

It may be that some people think about it consciously and deliberately and others rather unconsciously and dimly but that this conflict exists in the spirit of man today is certain. How it will be resolved I do not know. One thing that troubles me is this: people who understand one another more and more begin often enough to quarrel more and more. Nevertheless, it does not follow from this, that we should not try to understand one another. That would amount to limiting oneself completely and that is something which really cannot be done in the context of the modern World. Therefore, it becomes essential that we try to understand one another in the right way. The right way is important. The right approach, the friendly approach is important, because a friendly approach brings a friendly response. I have not the shadow of a doubt that it is a fundamental rule of human life that, if the approach is good, the response is good. If the approach is bad, the response is likely to be bad, too. So if we approach our fellow human beings or countries in a friendly way, with our minds and hearts open and prepared to accept whatever good comes to them—and that does not mean surrendering something that we consider of essential value to truth or to our own genius—then we shall be led only towards understanding but the right type of understanding.

THE ETERNAL SILENCE OF THESE INFINITE CROWDS

NIRAD C. CHAUDHARI

When visiting in England, I was almost always accompanied by an English friend, and, if not I was furnished with introductions. Therefore the question of worming my way through the notorious English reserve did not arise in my case. I was not wholly reassured, however, by the easy clearing of the first hurdle, and feared that difficulties might crop up at a later stage, for among us in India the coldness comes after and not before the introduction. It is practised in the interest of a salutary peck order in the upper strata of our society. But in England I came across no chilliness or formality, and was never put in my place even by important people.

Among us a gregarious life is not just contented and speechless adjacence as among cattle and the English people; it is a demonstrative exhibition of kindness as well as bad temper accompanied by a good deal of sound. In India heartiness is found more in the public intercourse of men than in private social relations. Moreover, for us noise is as essential a condition of cheerfulness as is the warmth of the sun.

For this reason I was not surprised to read a very angry letter published in one of our newspapers shortly after my return from abroad, in which the writer, a countryman of mine, complained about the silent habits of the English people. He wrote with burning hatred of their behaviour in the underground trains where they could think of nothing better to do than to bury their faces in their newspapers. A sailor perishing in the Arctic Ocean could not have felt more strongly about the icebergs.

I had heard about this habit before I went to England, but to meet the silence at first hand was a wholly novel experience. To me it seemed that not even their forums and agoras could be associated with characteristic sounds. Life in London, even in the most crowded street, seemed like a film of pre-talkie days. I had an uncanny sensation when I saw unending streams of people going along Oxford Street, and heard no sound. As they moved into the underground stations they looked like long lines of ants going into their holes. When after living in the bazaars of India for years I saw a sight like that, it was only natural that I should paraphrase Pascal and cry out : 'The eternal silence of these infinite crowds frightens me !'

I met the same silence when, from the streets, I went into the pubs or restaurants. Both can be crowded at lunch time. But I hear no conversation. In India, on the contrary, such places would be buzzing or even booming with talk. Speaking of the clubs, though regarded as centres of social life, they are perhaps the most silent places of all. One evening, when dining at a club, I tried in my innocence to open a conversation across the table, and I admired the skill with which the intrusion was fended off without the slightest suggestion of discourtesy.

But Englishmen have heard so much about their habits of silence from foreigners that they will see nothing new in my experience. They have heard the comment mostly from Frenchmen and other Europeans, and so can have no conception of the contrast they present to our ways in India. It is this contrast rather than the general fact of the silence which I wish to bring home, and as it happens I am particularly qualified to do so, because never having had a car I have always travelled by bus or tram, than which there are no better places to observe the public behaviour of a nation. The transport system of Delhi, which is owned by the Government and in which I have gone about for more than fifteen years, is very illuminating in this respect.

In the buses of Delhi all of us make use of one another for bodily comfort. In northern India people have very great difficulty in keeping steady in moving vehicles, and therefore they lean against one another or put their arms round a fellow-passenger. Nobody is so ill-natured as to mind being used as a cushion, and if anyone with a wholly alien notion of private ownership in respect of his body objects, he is asked in offended tones. 'What harm is there in it, you are not a woman ?' Again, if anyone wants to know the time and has not got a watch he simply takes up the left hand of another passenger and looks at his wrist-watch. I wear mine on the under side, and therefore I have my wrist twisted.

The buses are also full of conversation not only on public topics but also on embarrassingly private ones and not only between acquaintances but also between people who have never met before. Among the former the jokes are loud and hearty, and they are also permissible between total strangers. One day a fellow-passenger looked at my large sola topee and remarked that it was heavier than my whole body, and when I replied that it was no bigger than his turban he said that he hoped I was not offended at his joke.

Another day I even had an anxious inquiry about my health. In the hot season I sometimes get an irritation at the back of my neck, especially because I wear a collar and tie even then, and this makes me jerk my head and even perk it like a bird. Last summer I had an attack of this and when travelling in the bus, I suddenly heard the gentleman sitting next to me asking me in English, 'Is it habit or is it disease ?' As I was somewhat surprised by the question and could not at first understand what it was about, he repeated the query. I asked in my turn, 'What is habit or disease ?' Then the gentleman mimicked me exactly and said, 'This'. I was bound in common politeness to reply,

'I suppose it is habit'. 'I thought so too', he rejoined. 'You have done this too many times, and it has now become a habit, and habit as you know is second nature'. 'So it is, so it is,' I said in an embarrassed manner.

The passengers also help one another about the best way to get to a destination, because not infrequently the conductor has no clear idea of the topography of Delhi, and they often give contradictory directions, each maintaining that his is the right one. So far as newspaper reading is concerned, the fellow-passengers never snatch away anybody's paper, but they take the pages he is not reading, in the most polite manner, and distribute them among themselves. These are, however, scrupulously returned. Books are often tugged at. One day a fellow-passenger pulled hard at an edition of the *Gita* I was holding in my hand, and when I did not let go, but objected, he said angrily, 'You have got a holy book in your hand and you are behaving like this! I don't want your book'. And he did make a pariah of me.

I have the habit of leaving my seat and waiting at the door of the bus so as to be able to get down as soon as it comes to the stop instead of keeping it waiting as most of us do. But when the others see me doing this, they cry out in their anxiety, 'Please have patience'. Some even catch hold of my coat-tails or grip the arm to prevent me from moving. They also help in more exceptional circumstances. One day I found that I had only one bad rupee with me, and the conductor would not take it. In such a situation it is the custom with us to appeal to the 'general will' of the passengers. As I did not do that, a fellow-passenger snatched the coin from my hand, looked at it, and said, 'It is bad, but don't worry, I am going to exchange it for a good one'. And he took out a one rupee note, gave it to me, and put my bad rupee in his pocket. I was so amazed that I could not prevent him.

All sorts of other incidents happen, which make the bus in

Delhi a microcosm of our national life. On one occasion I saw a hysterical young woman trying to commit suicide by jumping out of a window, and being pulled back by her husband. There are quarrels, sometimes verbal, sometimes involving the limbs not only between a passenger and another passenger, or a passenger and the conductor, but also between the conductor and the driver. One day the two quarrelled and came to blows and then the driver got down in a huff and went off into Edward Park, to lie down on the grass. He did not come back until the whole body of passengers had shouted their entreaties to him for some time.

What takes place at the stops is even more out of the ordinary by Western standards, and I shall relate only one of my experiences. It should be remembered that in the capital of India the buses on certain routes come at intervals of twenty minutes or more, and that they are also irregular. I was waiting for my bus on one of the routes, and there came along an elderly gentleman with his family. He asked me if he could go to Red Fort from the stop, and when I said that he could, he thanked me profusely, and gave the information that he was a visitor to the town. He pointed to a young girl in the party and said, 'That is my daughter, she is in her B.A. class, and I am thinking now of her marriage'. Then he introduced his son to me too. After that he went on to say that they were coming from the house of Pandit Jawaharlal Nehru, where they had his Darshan, that is to say, were present at his ceremonial appearance before visitors. Continuing in this communicative vein, he informed me that the last time he had come to Delhi was two years ago, and that, he added with a shy smile, was over a lawsuit with his father.

I could hardly remain indifferent to the raising of such a topic. Seeing that I was interested he went to the trouble of explaining the whole affair. Of course, he spoke throughout in

English, and I shall give his exact words so far as I can remember them.

'You see,' he began, 'my mother died some years ago, and my father, who was old at the time, took a concubine. My brothers and I did not mind this at all, but after some time he brought this lady into the house, which we could not pass over. So my brothers and I went up to him and said, "Revered father, you cannot do that. You may, of course, associate with the lady, but you cannot bring her into our ancestral house where we, your sons, live with our children." Upon this my father got very angry and shouted, "Nothing doing! I shall disinherit the whole lot of you". We replied that he could not do that either. So it went to the courts. But the judge advised me to settle the matter out of court.'

At this point the bus came into view and I prepared to move. The gentleman surprised me, however, by asking for my name and address. Upon my inquiring the reason, he replied that he wanted to send me some mangoes from his own orchard and they were very good. I replied, 'Thank you very much. But there is really no occasion for it'.

'No, Sir', he rejoined with great warmth of feeling, 'it is no trouble whatever. You have given me the pleasure of your company and conversation, and I want to show my gratitude for it.' But the bus had come along and I had to jump into it, without being able to bring the matter to a more graceful conclusion.

It is this *Comedie humaine*, this large-hearted wiping out of the distinction between public and private affairs, this craving for sympathy in widest commonalty spread, that make us recoil from the dreariness of the public behaviour of the English people.

NO MAN IS AN ISLAND

MINOO MASANI

We had a peep into the future and saw how, if men are intelligent, they will merge all their states and their empires into a World Union or Federation. With that we seem to have come to the end of the exciting story of our growing human family. What then remains?

The answer is that the setting up of a World Federation is not the end or goal of human advance. It is in fact only a beginning—a means to a higher end. That goal we may describe—a freer, a fuller and a richer life for each human being, permitting the expression and the growth of his or her personality.

If today we know more than we did a few thousand years ago, if we are not so afraid as we were once of the forces of Nature (though we still are almost as afraid of one another), if we have learnt to relieve physical pain, if we have to work a little less hard, if perhaps we are a wee bit more reasonable, it is the result of centuries and centuries of mutual aid, of cooperation between larger and larger groups of men. It is because human beings have followed, not all the time nor very faithfully, the advice given in a verse to be found in one of the old Sanskrit books:

For the family sacrifice the individual, for the community the family, for the country the community and for the soul the whole world.

The World Federation of tomorrow or the day after will be the culmination of this process, but it will not automatically guarantee further progress. 'If the whole world were organized into a single State,' says one writer, 'yet mankind might be worse off under its sway, in the real essentials of human life, than if they were painted savages....We have always first to ask, "What kind of government?"··What kind of common life will it provide or allow to its citizens?"'

There are other people who say: 'What does it matter what kind of government there is, so long as it is efficient?" One such was the English poet, Alexander Pope, who wrote.

For forms of government let fools contest;
Whate'er is best administered is best.

Which may be a foolish thing to say, because who is to decide what is good government? One man may say that the present government of any given country is good, another may say it is rotten. It is a matter of opinion or point of view.

Are then there no tests by which you and I may judge whether any particular kind of government is good or bad? Are there no requirements we may ask a future world government to satisfy?

There are, I think, two such tests. The first is that government should serve 'the greatest good of the greatest number'; that is, it should be so organised as to give the people the nicest homes, the best food, the greatest comfort, the finest education and the greatest amount of leisure possible for recreation and for the creation and enjoyment of beautiful things.

The second test of good government is that it should at the same time give the largest amount of freedom to every man and woman and should treat their personalities with respect and sympathy, and act only with their consent. Since only the wearer knows where the shoe pinches, it means that the people should decide what kind of political shoe they choose to wear. That is democracy—which that great President of the United States of America, Abraham Lincoln, described as 'government of the people, by the people, and for the people'.

'Liberty,' said Lord Acton, the historian, 'is not a means to a higher political end. It is itself the highest political end'. Which means that without self-government there can be no lasting possibility of good government.

The big problem of government in our century is to reconcile the interests of society as a whole with the liberty of the individual, to make sure that one does not destroy the other. That government is the best which strikes a perfect balance between the two.

Throughout the world today people are faced with a choice between various kinds of governments. There are rival political doctors, each with his own brand of patent medicine, who guarantee to cure us of our ills if only we put ourselves under their treatment. And poor Mr. Man-in-the-Sheet, whether he is in Bombay or Dublin or Stockholm or Rio de Janeiro, feels dreadfully puzzled and wonders which to choose.

Shall we be chemists for a little while and analyse these patent medicines? Let us see how they stand our two tests because, as citizens of the world, we have each of us to make our choice. By the time we have finished our analysis, we shall find that we can sort out these various brands of government into two main groups.

In the first kind, the individual citizen can think and say more or less what he likes. The government is responsible to the people and can be replaced by another if the majority of the people desire. In countries which belong to this group, which we may call democracies, the result generally is widespread education and enlightenment, a rising standard of living, and greater equality between different classes of people. That is not, however, the case in all such countries. In some of these, money power is strong and the gulf between a handful of rich people and the masses of the poor is wide. There is very little planning, and often a lot of waste. The results of following a democratic way of life are rather uneven, and vary widely from country to country. That is only natural since the success of the democratic way of life is dependent on the wisdom or stupidity of the common people who govern themselves. Each nation, it has been said, gets the kind of government it deserves.

When we turn to the other group of states, which we may call dictatorships, we find the governments have total control over the life of the people. Industries are owned and run by the state, and everything is planned in advance by the official. Right as the top of the state there is One Man. He orders everything. He dictates. The dictator's every whim must be obeyed. Any opposition to him is destroyed by force—by death. Like the kings of olden times, he can do no wrong. His officials obey him as soldiers obey a general. A common man may not speak or write or even think for himself. Now, if it were possible for such a system to yield results in increasing the prosperity and happiness of the people, there might *perhaps* be something to be said for it, though personally I would not like to live in such a state, nor I guess, would you? As it happens however, although the dictators claim omniscience and demand that all decisions should be left to them for the general good, none of the basic problems of our time has been solved in such states. Conditions of work and living show no improvement; equality is even more distant than before. Liberty, which has been bartered away in the vain hope of equality and security, is lost and nothing has been gained in return but more inequality and more fear.

So there we are. We must turn back to the first brand, inadequate and disappointing as it may sometimes be. History teaches us that there are no short cuts to the good life, which has to be earned and deserved by the people before it is achieved. We do want planning for a good life, but not at the cost of liberty. We must move forward to a better society as fast as we can, but that cannot be faster than people are ready to move—freely and of their own will.

How, you will ask, can such big steps forward be taken? Can they be achieved by violent wars and revolutions? There are many people who think so, and they are prepared to beat and kill others who won't swallow their special brand of the new order. There are also some wiser people—they are very few—who won't believe that by killing people you can make them wiser or more friendly! They don't think noble ends can be achieved by foul methods. Such were Buddha and Asoka and Jesus Christ. Such in our time and in our own country has been Mahatma Gandhi, whose weapons were non-violence and truth.

We often hear people say that most human beings have not yet evolved or grown up enough to stick to truth or non-violence. That is very true. Somebody has described the people of our time as possessing the powers of gods and the minds of school-children. Which only shows how grown-ups will put on airs! A Russian peasant put the same idea much better when he told the writer Maxim Gorki: 'You can fly in the air like birds and swim in the sea like fish, but you don't know how to walk upon the earth like men.'

Now, there is no need to get despondent at the fact that human beings lack the intelligence as yet to know their real interests. We must not forget that the human race is still very, very young. C. E. M. Joad, in his delightful little *Story of Civilization*, has computed that if we reckon the whole past of living creatures on the earth as one hundred years, the entire past of Man works out at one month, and during that month there has been civilization for only seven or eight hours. He also points out that while there has been little time for us to learn things so far, there will be oceans of time in which to learn better. Because, while Man's civilized past has lasted seven or eight hours, his future (till the sun grows too cold or too hot to maintain life on the earth) is estimated on the same scale at a hundred thousand years!

So people have to be educated 'to walk upon the earth like men' and to take the next step forward. We find here and there some peoples who were very warlike once upon a time but have now grown up enough to be mild and peace loving. Such for instance, are the Swedes and the Swiss. It is necessary that people all over the world should become educated like that. If they don't learn their lessons in time, they will go on having one terrible war after another until—like the dinosaur and the brontosaurus who would go on fighting amongst themselves—the human species becomes extinct.

How is this to be avoided? By people being taught to think freely and to think new thoughts. Some clever person once pointed out that if everybody had always thought the same as his parents we should all of us still be savages!

Where do you and I come into this picture? We come in because as a seventeenth-century English poet, John Donne, put it (in the spelling of the time which I am leaving untouched):

> No man is an Island, intire of it self; every man is a peice of the Continent, a part of the maine; if a Clod bee washed away by the Sea, Europe is the lesse, as well as if a Promontorie were as well as if a Mannor of thy friends or of thine owne were; any mans death diminishes me, because I am involved in Mankinde; And therefore never send to know for whom the bell tolls; It tolls for thee.

We are all members of one human family and must stand or fall together. There is no life possible for us except though the medium of society—that medium which 'supplies nourishment to the growing baby, equips it with the signs of language and the symbols of association, prepares it by cultural habitation to eat this food and reject that poison, to believe this truth and turn aside from that error.'

You and I have a part to play in this forward march, in this long pilgrimage of Man. Each of us can decide whether he or she will lead in the vanguard or be one of the many stagglers in the rear.

The process that has made people like you and me out of the ape-man in some fifty thousand years has by no means come to an end. It has to continue until men and women become something like the gods and goddesses they have so far imagined and worshipped. That is not just a day-dream. Because, just as men have not always been men but have gradually evolved out of a different kind of creature, so men need not always be men but could gradually evolve into yet different beings.

The spirit of Man has faced all kinds of dangers and his growing intelligence has slowly and painfully surmounted all the obstacles that have come in his way. Each one of us is a custodian of a little particle of that spirit and that intellgence. We have to guard and preserve it against all attempts to take it away from us. We have to speak the truth as we see it, even if all around us there is falsehood and darkness.

STORIES

THE BABUS OF NAYANJORE

RABINDRANATH TAGORE

Once upon a time the Babus of Nayanjore were famous landlords. They were noted for their princely extravagance. They would tear off the rough border of their Dacca muslin, because it rubbed against their delicate skin. They would spend many thousands of rupees over the wedding of a kitten. And on a certain grand occasion it is alleged that in order to turn night into day they lighted countless lamps and showered silver threads from the sky to imitate sunlight.

Those were the days before the flood. The flood came. The line of succession among these old world Babus, with their lordly habits, could not continue for long. Like a lamp, with too many wicks burning, the oil flared away quickly, and the light went out.

Kailas Babu, our neighbour, is the last flicker of this extinct magnificence. Before he grew up, his family had very nearly burned itself out. When his father died, there was one dazzling outburst of funeral extravagance, and then insolvency. The property was sold to liquidate the debt. What little ready money was left was altogether insufficient to keep up the ancestral splendours.

Kailas Babu left Nayanjore and came to Calcutta. His son did not remain long in this world of faded glory. He died, leaving behind him an only daughter.

In Calcutta we are Kailas Babu's neighbours. Curiously enough our own family history is just the opposite of his. My father made his money by his own exertions, and prided himself on never spending a penny more than was necessary. His clothes were those of a working man, and his hands also. He never had any inclination to earn the title of Babu by extravagant display; and I, his only son, am grateful to him for that. He gave me the very best education, and I was able to make my way in the world. I am not ashamed of the fact that I am a self-made man. Crisp notes in my safe are dearer to me than a long pedigree in an empty family chest.

I believe this was why I disliked seeing Kailas Babu drawing his heavy cheques on the public credit from the bankrupt bank of his ancient Babu reputation. I used to fancy that he looked down on me, because my father had earned money by manual labour.

I ought to have noticed that no one but myself showed any vexation towards Kailas Babu. Indeed it would have been difficult to find an old man who did less harm than he. He was always ready with his kindly little acts of courtesy in times of sorrow or joy. He would join in all the ceremonies and religious observances of his neighbours. His familiar smile would greet young and old alike. His politeness in asking details about domestic affairs was untiring. The friends who met him in the street were ready perforce to be button-holed, while a long string of remarks of this kind followed one another from his lips :

'I am delighted to see you, my dear friend. Are you quite well ? How is Sashi ? And Dada—is he all right ? Do you know, I've only just heard that Madhu's son has got fever. How is he? Have you heard ? And Hari Charan Babu—I have not seen him for a long time,—I hope he is not ill. What's the matter with Rakhal ? And er—er, how are the ladies of your family ?"

Kailas Babu was neat and spotless in his dress on all occasions though his supply of clothes was sorely limited. Every day he used to air his shirts and vests and coats and trousers carefully, and put them out in the sun, along with his bed-quilt, his pillow-case, and the small carpet on which he always sat. After airing them he would shake them, and brush them, and put them carefully away. His little bits of furniture made his small room presentable, and hinted that there was more in reserve if needed. Very often, for want of a servant he would shut up his house for a while. Then he would iron out his shirts and linen, and do other little menial tasks. He would then open his door and receive his friends again.

Though Kailas Babu, as I have said, had lost all his land, he had still some family heirlooms left. There was a silver cruet for sprinkling scented water, a filigree box for otto-of-roses, a small gold salver, a costly antique shawl, and the old-fashioned ceremonial dress and ancestral turban. These he had rescued with the greatest difficulty from the money-lenders' clutches. On every suitable occasion he would bring them out in state, and thus try to save the world-famed dignity of the Babus of Nayanjore. At heart the most modest of men, in his daily speech he regarded it as a sacred offering, due to his rank, to give free play to his family pride. His friends would encourage this, with kindly good-humour, and it gave them great amusement.

The people of the neighbourhood soon learnt to call him their Thakur Dada. They would flock to his house and sit with him for hours together. To prevent his incurring any expense, one or other of his friends would bring him tobacco and say: 'Thakur Dada, this morning some tobacco was sent to me from Gaya. Do try it and see how you like it.'

Thakur Dada would smoke it and say it was excellent. He would then proceed to tell of a certain exquisite tobacco which they once smoked in the old days at Nayanjore that cost a guinea an ounce.

'I wonder,' he used so say, 'if any one would like to try it now. I have some left, and can get it at once.

Every one knew that, if they asked for it, then somehow or other the key of the cupboard would be missing; or else Ganesh, his old family servant, had put it away somewhere.

'You never can be sure,' he would add, 'where things go to

when servants are about. Now, this Ganesh of mine,—I can't tell you what a fool he is, but I haven't the heart to dismiss him.'

Ganesh, for the credit of the family, was quite ready to bear all the blame without a word.

One of the company usually said at this point : 'Never mind, Thakur Dada. Please don't trouble to look for it. The tobacco we're smoking will do quite well. The other would be too strong.'

Then Thakur Dada would be relieved and settle down again, and the talk would go on.

When his guests got up to go away, Thakur Dada would accompany them to the door and say to them on the door-step : 'Oh by the way, when are you all coming to dine with me ?'

One or other of us would answer : 'Not just yet, Thakur Dada, not just yet. We'll fix a day later.'

'Quite right,' he would answer. 'Quite right. We had much better wait till the rains come. It's too hot now. And a grand dinner, such as I should want to give you, would upset us in weather like this.'

But when the rains did come, every one was very careful not to remind him of his promise. If the subject was brought up, some friend would suggest gently, that it was very inconvenient to get about when the rains were so severe, and therefore it would be much better to wait till they were over. Thus the game went on.

Thakur Dada's poor house was much too small for his position, and we used to condole with him about it. His friends would assure him they quite understood his difficulties; it was next to impossible to get a decent house in Calcutta. Indeed, they had all been looking out for years for a house to suit him. But, I need hardly add, no friend had been foolish enough to find one. Thakur Dada used to say, with a sign of resignation:

'Well, well, I suppose I shall have to put up with this house after all.' Then he would add with a genial smile: 'But, you know, I could never bear to be away from my friends. I must be near you. That really compensates for everything.'

Somehow I felt all this very deeply indeed. I suppose the real reason was that, when a man is young, stupidity appears to him the worst of crimes. Kailas Babu was not really stupid. In ordinary business matters every one was ready to consult him. But with regard to Nayanjore his utterances certainly seemed void of commonsense. Since, out of amused affection for him, no one contradicted his impossible statements, he refused to keep them within bounds. When people recounted in his hearing the glorious history of Nayanjore, with absurd exaggerations, he would accept all they said with the utmost gravity, and never doubted even in his dreams, that any one could disbelieve it.

When I sit down and try to analyse the thoughts and feelings that I had towards Kailas Babu, I see that there was a still deeper reason for my dislike; which I shall now explain.

Though I am the son of a rich man, and might have wasted time at college, my industry was such that I took my M.A. degree at Calcutta University when quite young. My moral character was flawless. In addition, my outward appearance was so handsome, that if I were to call myself beautiful, it might be thought a mark of self esteem but could not be considered an untruth.

There could be no question that I was regarded by parents generally as a very eligible match among the young men of Bengal. I myself was quite clear on the point and had determined to obtain my full value in the marriage market. When I pictured my choice, I had before my mind's eye a wealthy father's only daughter, extremely beautiful and highly educated. Proposals came pouring in to me from far and near; large sums in cash were offered. I weighed these offers with rigid impartiality in the delicate scales of my own estimation. But there was no one fit to be my partner. I became convinced with the poet Bhabavuti, that

> In this world's endless time and boundless space
> One *may* be born at last to match my sovereign grace.

But in this puny modern age, and this contracted space of modern Bengal, it was doubtful whether the peerless creature existed.

Meanwhile my praises were sung in many tunes, and in different metres, by designing parents.

Whether I was pleased with their daughters or not, this worship which they offered was never unpleasing. I used to regard it as my proper due, because I was so good. We are told that when the gods withhold their boons from mortals they still expect their worshippers to pay them fervent honour and are angry if it is withheld. I had that divine expectancy strongly developed.

I have already mentioned that Thakur Dada had an only grand-daughter. I had seen her many times; but had never thought her beautiful. No idea had ever entered my mind that she would be a possible partner for me. All the same it seemed quite certain to me that some day or other Kailas Babu would offer her, with all due worship, as an oblation at my shrine. Indeed,—this was the inner secret of my dislike,—I was thoroughly annoyed that he had not done so already.

I heard that Thakur Dada had told his friends that the Babus of Nayanjore never craved a boon. Even if the girl remained unmarried, he would not break the family tradition. It was this arrogance of his that made me angry. My indignation smouldered for some time. But I remained perfectly silent and bore it with the utmost patience, because I was so good.

As lightning accompanies thunder, so in my character a flash of humour was mingled with the mutterings of my wrath. It was, of course, impossible for me to punish the old man merely in order to give vent to my rage; and for a long time I did nothing at all. But suddenly one day such an amusing plan came into my head, that I could not resist the temptation to carry into effect.

I have already said that many of Kailas Babu's friends used to flatter the old man's vanity without stint. One, who was a retired Government servant, had told him that whenever he saw the Chota Lāt Sahib he asked for the latest news about the Babus of Nayanjore and the Chota Lāt had been heard to say that in all Bengal the only really respectable families were those of the Maharaja of Cossipore and the Babus of Nayanjore. When the monstrous falsehood was told to Kailas Babu he was very proud and often repeated the story. And wherever after that he met this Government servant in company he would ask, among other things :

'Oh ! er—by the way, how is the Chota Lāt Sahib ? Quite well, did you say ? Ah yes, I am so delighted to hear it ! And the dear Mem Sahib, is she quite well too ? Ah, yes ! and the little children,—are they quite well also ? Ah yes ! that's very good news ! Be sure and give them my compliments when you see them.'

Kailas Babu frequently expressed his intention of going some day and paying a visit to the Lāt Sahib. But it may be taken for granted that many Chota Lāts and Burra Lāts also would come and go, and much water would flow under the Hooghly bridges, before the family coach of Nayanjore would be furbished up to take Kailas Babu to Government House.

One day I took him aside and whispered to him : 'Thakur Dada, I was at the Levee yesterday, and the Chota Lāt Sahib happened to mention the Babus of Nayanjore. I told him that Kailas Babu had come to town. Do you know, he was terribly hurt because you hadn't called ? He told me he was going to put etiquette on one side and pay you a private visit this very afternoon.'

Anybody else would have seen through this plot of mine in a

moment. And, if it had been directed against another person, Kailas Babu would have understood the joke. But after all that he had heard from his friend the Government servant, and after all his own exaggerations, a visit from the Lieutenant-Governor seemed the most natural thing in the world. He became very nervous and excited at my news. Each detail of the coming visit exercised him greatly,—most of all his own ignorance of English. How on earth was that difficulty to be met? I told him there was no difficulty at all; it was an aristocratic foible not to know English; besides, the Lieutenant-Governor always brought an interpreter with him, and he had expressly mentioned that this visit was to be private.

About midday, when most of our neighbours were at work, and the rest were asleep, a carriage and pair stopped before the lodging of Kailas Babu. Two flunkeys in livery came up the stairs, and announced in a loud voice : 'The Chota Lât Sahib!' Kailas Babu was ready, waiting for him, in his old-fashioned ceremonial robes and ancestral turban, with Ganesh by his side, dressed for the occasion in his master's best clothes.

When the Chota Lât Sahib was announced, Kailas Babu ran panting, puffing and trembling to the door, and led in with repeated salaams, a friend of mine, in disguise. As he did so, he bowed low at each step and walked backwards as well as he could. He had spread his old family shawl over a hard wooden chair on which he asked the Lât Sahib to be seated. He then made a high-flown speech in Urdu, the ancient Court language of the Sahibs, and presented on the golden salver a string of gold *mohurs*, the last relics of his broken fortune. The old family servant Ganesh, with an expression of awe bordering on terror, stood behind with the scent-sprinkler, simply drenching the Lât Sahib, and touching him gingerly from time to time with the otto-of-roses from the filigree box.

Kailas Babu repeatedly expressed his regret at not being able to receive His Honour Bahadur with all the ancestral magnificence of his family estate at Nayanjore. There he could have welcomed him with due ceremonial. But in Calcutta, he said, he was a mere stranger and sojourner,—in fact, a fish out of water.

My friend, with his tall silk hat on, very gravely nodded. I need hardly say that according to English custom the hat ought to have been removed inside the room. But my friend dared not take it off for fear of detection, and Kailas and his old servant Ganesh were sublimely unconscious of this breach of etiquette.

After a ten minutes' interview, which on his part consisted chiefly of nodding the head, my friend rose to depart. The two flunkeys in livery, as had been planned beforehand, carried off in state the string of gold *mohurs*, the gold salver, the gold ancestral shawl, the silver scent-sprinkler, and the otto-of-roses filigree box; they placed them ceremoniously in the carriage. Kailas Babu regarded this as the usual habit of a Chota Lāt Sahib.

I was watching all the while from the next room. My sides were aching with suppressed laughter. When I could hold myself in no longer, I rushed into a room further off, suddenly to discover, in a corner, a young girl sobbing as though her heart would break. When she heard my uproarious laughter she stood tense in passion, flashing the lightning of her big dark eyes in mine and said with a tear-choked voice : 'Tell me ! What harm has my grandfather done to you ! Why have you come to deceive him ? Why have you come here ? Why—'

She could say no more. She covered her face with her hands and broke into sobs.

My laughter stopped instantly. It had never occurred to me that there was anything but a supremely funny joke in this act of mine, and here I discovered that I had given the cruellest pain to this tender little heart. All the ugliness of my cruelty rose up to condemn me. I slunk out of the room in silence, like a whipped dog.

Hitherto I had only looked upon Kusum, the grand-daughter

of Kailas Babu, as a somewhat worthless commodity in the marriage market, waiting in vain to attract a husband. But now I found, with surprise, that in the corner of that room a human heart was beating.

The whole night through I had very little sleep. My mind was in a tumult. Very early next morning, I took all those stolen goods back to Kailas Babu's lodgings, to hand them over in secret to the servant Ganesh. I waited outside the door, and, finding no one, went upstairs to Kailas Babu's room. I heard from the passage Kusum asking her grandfather in the most winning voice : 'Dada, dearest, do tell me all that the Chota Lāt Sahib said to you yesterday. Don't leave out a single word. I am dying to hear it all over again.'

And Dada needed no encouragement. His face beamed with pride as he related all the compliments that the Lāt Sahib had been good enough to utter concerning the ancient families of Nayanjore. The girl was seated before him looking up into his face, and listening with rapt attention. She was determined, out of love for the old man, to play her part so well as to allow no suspicion to enter his mind.

My heart was deeply touched, and tears came to my eyes. I stood there in silence in the passage, while Thakur Dada finished his account, with embellishments, of the Chota Lāt Sahib's wonderful visit. When at last, he left the room, I took the stolen goods, laid them at the feet of the girl and came away without a word.

Later in the day I called again to see him. According to our ugly modern custom, I had been in the habit of making no greeting at all to this old man when I came into the room. But today I made a low bow and touched his feet I am convinced the old man thought that the coming of the Chota Lāt Sahib to his house was the cause of my new politeness. He was very much gratified by it, and benign serenity shone from his eyes. His friends had looked in, and he had already begun to tell again at full length the story of the Lieutenant-Governer's visit with still further adornments of a most fantastic kind. The story of the interview was already becoming epic, both in quality and in length.

When the other visitors had taken their leave, I humbly made my proposal to the old man. I told him that, 'though I could never for a moment hope to be worthy of being received into such an illustrious family in marriage, yet ...etc., etc.'

When I made my proposal clear, the old man embraced me and broke out in an excess of joy : 'I am a poor man, and could never have expected such great good fortune.'

That was the first and last time in his life that Kailas Babu confessed his poverty. It was also the first and last time in his life that he forgot, if only for a single moment, the ancestral dignity of the Babus of Nayanjore.

THE BROTHERS

MULK RAJ ANAND

As they came into the waiting room of the Ayurvedic Doctor, Pandit Prakash Shastri, they almost looked like twin brothers, so completely did they resemble each other in their appearances. The only difference was that the hair of the elder of the two was greying on the temples.

But when the younger brother took a step forward and addressed the compounder of medicines, Shri Rajiner Shankar, through the small window of the wooden cabin, another difference between the two entrants became noticeable:

'We are Raj Brothers Jewellers, from near Opera House !... Tell Panditji we are in a hurry, so that he can call us quickly !'

This was said by Lalla Lekh Raj, the younger brother, in a tone which was at the apex of asininity from the first sound of his utterance. On hearing the injunction Lalla Hans Raj had winced slightly, looked furtively this side and that in order to see whether the other patient and their relations, waiting in the narrow cubicle further up, had noticed the strain of peremptory arrogance in his younger brother's voice.

Actually, some of the people in the waiting room, who were seated on nearby chairs looked up briefly, wriggled impatiently with the heat and the apprehension of further delay is being seen by the Doctor, if, indeed, the aggressive plea of the newcomer may secure him priority into the consulting room.

In the small waiting room with the big cane chairs there was hardly any room to 'throw a til seed', as it were.

Lalla Lekh Raj saw a girl of five seated on an armchair. He forthwith went up to the child and signified to her to get up by raising the forefinger of his right hand. The little girl looked to her mother for protection, but got up without waiting for advice. Whereupon Lalla Lekh Raj lowered his posterior into the vacated chair with the alacrity of the self-possessed Punjabi whose original bad manners had not been improved by the films from Hollywood.

The mother of the girl child looked askance at the intruder and then, meekly, with lowered eyes, pulled her daughter on to her lap.

During the enactment of this little drama, the elder brother, Lalla Hans Raj, who was the patient, stood quivering by the corner of the compounder's cabin. He was embarrassed by his brother's behaviour and did not know how to make amends. And he tried to interpret Lekh Raj's zeal to annex a chair as inspired by his brother's concern for him. In fact, he heard Lekh Raj say loudly:

'Ao, brother, come and sit down here...I will sit on the arm of the chair.'

By this time, the father of a boy of twelve had gathered his son unto himself from an upright office style chair near the entrance to the consulting room, and he indicated to Hans Raj the vacant seat.

Hans Raj took the seat, looking this side and that, through the fear of being thought as brazen as his brother Lekh Raj. He was no saint himself. But, since the carnage of the partition riots between India and Pakistan, through which he had emerged with his life, by lying under the bunk of a third class carriage pretending to be dead when the others were murdered, he had felt, growing in him, the circumspection of the human gesture which lay almost invisibly in his weak heart. All the other people in Bombay seemed to him to be made of some other stuff, as they 'kicked each other in the ditch' in the scramble of the great gold rush. And, especially his brother, who made him feel hot and cold with the pressure of his torso into quarrels over small gains, not only in business but even in a bargain with a vegetable seller. Somehow, in recent months, Lekh Raj had become more impatient than ever. For instance, he had said to him only yesterday that 'if the heart trouble is serious, and you can't come to the shop more than a few hours a day, won't it be better to have a partition of the family property—perhaps you would like to retire !' He, Hans Raj, had tried to look the other way and slightly out of breath, had sat down on the chair behind the counter, in order to avoid collapsing in a heap, there and then. And he had tried to discern some small haven of escape in his soul where he could rest on his precipitous journey between life and death. As he had not answered back, Lekh Raj had become more excited still. And, although unable to force the solution on his elder brother, who had founded the jewellery business with the investment of the gold he had resurrected from Lahore, the younger brother's face had become contorted and set, even as he had whispered: 'The taint of death is inauspicious—and customers seem to wither away on seeing a sick man in a shop, anyhow !' For a moment he, Hans Raj, had looked up and seen Lekh Raj's face.

It was, as the scriptures said 'like that of a demon, in delirium tremors and simultaneously in the agony of a scorpion bite, while possessed besides by the seven devils....With the onrush of such memories, the sick man sought to exorcize the bad thoughts, and excitement, and twitched slightly in the effort to settle down in the chair. He had hardly had time to master his feelings when the voice of Pandit Prakash Shastri announced: 'Next.' And before Hans Raj knew where he was, Lekh Raj had pressed down upon him, lifted his right arm and dragged him into the consulting-room, leaving the other patients to dissolve into sweat with red upturned faces in the grip of consternation and wonder at the effrontery of the newcomers.

Pandit Prakash Shastri preserved an imperturbable calm in the face of the provocation offered by the queue breakers. His wise, lean face seemed to have been refined by the self-mastery of the passions, which good Doctors are forced to employ as a part of the process of healing the anguish and pain of sickness. The bald head alone reflected certain authority and prestige before which the patients remained subdued.

But Lekh Raj was not subdued. He merely considered the sheen on top of the Doctor's head funny. And, though he could not mock at the healer openly, he invented the first hyperbole so dramatically as to leave no doubt in Pandit Prakash Shastri's mind as to what he thought of him.

'Panditji, you are a great Ayurvedic physician ! And your miraculous cures are the talk of the whole of Hindustan !', began Lekh Raj, convinced that every man has his own vanity.

'I am trying to restore the ancient system of Indian medicine to its former position,' Pandit Prakash Shastri answered to objectify his mission and to recover from his personal embarrassment.

'We have heard of your miracles from all the great film stars who come to our shop for their jewellery,' Lalla Lekh Raj persisted. But he had not reckoned on the humility of this particular physician.

'I charge the film stars very heavy fees.' Pandit Prakash Shastri said. 'That's why they like me, perhaps. You know they take three to five lakhs black and fifty thousand white. So they can spend the cash and keep my hospital going. Also, they would not believe in a Doctor who gives medicines free.'

'I hope,' said Lekh Raj in a panic, 'that you won't charge us what you charge these people, because we are only shopkeepers who have built up a small business since we came here after the partition.'

'Panditji will charge according to his wishes,' intervened Hans Raj, the patient, with a little show of impatience. He did not want any talk of fees before he had been able to explain his illness. And he did not wish to ruin the treatment through the gaucheness of his younger brother's blunderous speech.

'I would like to know a little about you,' the Doctor said demurely. 'I could not understand much on the telephone.'

'My elder brother,' began Lekh Raj.

'Let the patient explain,' said Pandit Prakash Shastri firmly. This made the patient blush for shame at his younger brother's irrepressible impetuosity. But after swallowing a choking breath, he said:

'Panditji, I tramped from studio to studio to canvass orders, after I set up business here twelve years ago. This climate is not good for Punjabis—its humidity is killing...And then there were all kind of difficulties. The film people don't often pay cash. And there are law suits and...Anyhow, I seem to have a heart which...But, being used to a walk every morning to the Ravi and back, I thought I had a good constitution and I neglected the illness. Then, one day, about five years ago, I suddenly began to sweat all over, while I was in Andheri. I felt pain between my ribs. And I was taken to a Marhatta Doctor in Ghodbunder Road...Then, about a year ago, both of us were going on business to Poona and in an accident—'

'I suppose your younger brother was driving,' cut in the Doctor.

'Panditji,' said Lekh Raj concerned, 'It was a pure accident. I am a good driver, though I only learnt three years ago. I was behind another car. Beyond us on the right-hand side was a stationary lorry. A jeep station wagon from behind the lorry barged right into us, imagining that there was no car behind the first one which had gone ahead of us.

'I did not feel anything immediately,' said the patient Hans Raj. 'In fact, we went to the police at Panvel to report... But, afterwards, I felt I was going to have a heart attack. So I went to hospital from the police station and just lay down.

The Doctors there mistook ths injury on my head for the cause of the pain in my chest...'

'And I suppose your other Doctors have been giving you western drugs to murder you slowly and put you to permanent rest,' put in Pandit Prakash Shastri.

'I have taken him to many Doctors' said Lekh Raj.

'But they all charge big fees and...'

'The American medicines don't suit me, Panditji,' said Hans Raj. 'That is why I have come to you...'

'Acha, will you lie down on that table,' said Pandit Prakash Shastri. 'I believe in English style diagnosis, though I will give you indigenous medicines...And, perhaps—oh never mind... Your younger brother can stay...'

The patient lay down on the table.

The Doctor picked up his stethoscope and proceeded towards him.

Lalla Lekh Raj sat convulsed by the humiliation implicit in Pandit Prakash Shastri's unexpressed wish that he should withdraw from the consulting room. The pride of his uproused blood made his face red. And the gloomy shadow of his elder brother's possible recovery rose above the skilful hands of the Doctor, threatening all his plans for the future. The lord of pleasure danced over his head, stamping into his consciousness that all his life was tangled up. There was no easy way to the pinnacle of glory of which he had dreamed—to be equal to Nanubhai Jeweller and set up a store in Mahatma Gandhi Road...

After the Doctor had finished the examination, he returned to the chair behind the large table and began to write a prescription.

Hans Raj buttoned up his tunic and descended from the platform.

Lekh Raj looked from the one to the other, wishing to find an opening through which he might be able to make a breach into the atmosphere of cordiality which the Doctor had built up with his elder brother. The consulting room seemed to him to have been uplifted by the urge to master the Doctor's soul with a bribe for his wife.

'We have a beautiful antique piece—a Mughal necklace which has come down from Akbar Padshah through Raja Man Singh of Jaipur,' he began grandiloquently...'We would like to show it to you, Panditji, if you will accept it—'

'I don't take gold,' Pandit Prakash Shastri said priggishly. 'For me the bank notes are more useful. I prefer a cheque because I pay Income Tax...But do not pay until the cure has begun...And here is the prescription. Rajinder Shankar there will cash it for you in ten minutes...Lala Hans Raj, take this, and I would like to see you again next week—same time...'

Lala Hans Raj took the paper and proceeded to go out.

Lalla Lekh Raj sat where he was, toying with the evening paper, *Free Press Bulletin*.

When his brother had left, Lalla Lekh Raj ducked his head into his chest, then coughed, twisted his mouth into the grimace of *bonhomie*, and tried to speak.

The Doctor averted his eyes from the man and hoped he would spit out what he had to say and go. His intimate insight into the impure face of his client assured him the man was struggling within him to speak.

'Panditji,' Lalla Lekh Raj breathed haltingly, 'Do you not believe in mercy—I mean, my brother is suffering so much... And life is not worth living in our household, although we have no shortage of wealth...Can't you make God call him to himself by some medicine which may slowly burn away his pain—and...'

The hidden river of compassion in the Doctor which was the source of his love for healing, suddenly turned on its side and he stormed :

'Lalla Lekh Raj, you have no shame, but your soul will be

tormented if you go on talking and hoping like that...Go and look after your brother.'

'But Panditji ! Lekh Raj protested.

The Doctor rose from his chair from the infinite uproar of the river in him.

* * *

The patient Lalla Hans Raj did not come back at the same time, on the same day, next week.

Nor did he return the week after, or the week after, or the week after.

About the end of the fifth week the patient's younger brother, Lalla Lekh Raj, came and, without waiting for his turn, barged in to announce that his elder brother, the 'saintly Lalla Hans Raj' had expired in his sleep soon after his visit to Panditji....'

'As my brother did not pay you the fees, I have brought that antique piece, the Mughal necklace, for your wife...'

The storm in Pandit Prakash Shastri's soul had abated during the time with the routine of attending to his patients. He merely said whimsically :

'May I condole with you on the passing away of your saintly brother...And may I ask you to forgive me for not accepting the antique piece, the Mughal necklace...Gold can be poisoned with a smear of arsenic. Anyhow my wife died long ago. Perhaps you will give it to your sister-in-law, the wife of the deceased patient. Since you will give nothing else to her...'

COMPANIONS

RAJA RAO

Alas till now I did not know
My guide and Fate's guide are one.

—HAFIZ

It WAS a serpent such as one sees only at a fair, long and many-coloured and swift in riposte when the juggler stops his music. But it had a secret of its own which none knew except Moti Khan who brought him to the Fatehpur Sunday fair. The secret was: his fangs would lie without venom till the day Moti Khan should see the vision of the large white rupee, with the Kutub Minar on the one side and the face of the Emperor on the other. That day the fang would eat into his flesh and Moti Khan would only be a cospre of a man. Unless he find God.

For to tell you the truth, Moti Khan had caught him in the strangest of strange circumstances. He was one day going through the *sitaphul* wood of Rampur on a visit to his sister, and the day being hot and the sands all scorching and shiny, he lay down under a wild fig-tree, his turban on his face and his legs stretched across a stone. Sleep came like a swift descent of dusk, and after rapid visions of palms and hills and the dizzying sunshine, he saw a curious thing. A serpent came in the form of a man, opened its mouth, and through the most queer twistings of his face, declared he was Pandit Srinath Sastri of Totepur, who, having lived at the foot of the Goddess Lakshamma for a generation or more, one day in the ecstacy of his vision he saw her, the benign Goddess straight and supple, offering him two boons. He thought of his falling house and his mortgaged ancestral lands and said, without a thought, 'A bagful of gold and liberation from the cycle of birth and death'. 'And gold you shall have', said the Goddess, 'but for your greed, you shall be born a serpent in your next life before reaching liberation. For gold and wisdom go in life like soap and oil. Go and be born a juggler's serpent. And when you have made the hearts of many men glad with the ripple and swing of your shining flesh, and you have gone like a bird amidst shrieking children, only to swing round their legs and to swing out to the amusement of them all, when you have climbed old men's shoulders and hung down them chattering like a squirrel, when you have thrust your hood at the virgin and circled round the marrying couples; when you have gone through the dreams of pregnant women and led the seekers to the top of the Mount of Holy Beacon, then your sins will be worn out like the quern with man's grindings and your flesh will catch fire like the will-o-the-wisp and disappear into the world of darkness where men await the birth to come. The juggler will be a basket-maker and Moti Khan is his name. In a former life he sought God but in this he sits on the lap of a concubine. Wending his way to his sister's for the birth of her son, he will sleep in the *sitaphul* woods. Speak to him. And he will be the vehicle of your salvation'. Thus spoke the Goddess.

'Now, what do you say to that, Moti Khan?'

'Yes, I've been a sinner. But never thought I, God and Satan would become one. Who are you?'

'The very same serpent.'

'Your race has caused the fall of Adam.'

'I sat at the feet of Sri Lakshamma and fell into ecstasy. I am a brahmin.'

'You are strange.'

'Take me or I'll haunt you for this life and all lives to come.'

'Go, Satan !' shouted Moti Khan, and rising swift as a sword he started for his sister's house. He said to himself, 'I will think of my sister and her child. I will think only of them.' But leaves rustled and serpents came forth from the left and the right, blue ones and white ones and red ones and copper-coloured ones, long ones with short tails and short ones with bent tails, and serpents dropped from tree-tops and rock-edges, serpents hissed on the river sands. Then Moti Khan stood by the Rampur stream and said, Wretch ! Stop it. Come, I'll take you with me.' Then the serpents disappeared and so did the hissings, and hardly home, he took a basket and put it in a corner, and then he slept; and when he woke, a serpent had curled itself in the basket. Moti Khan had a *pungi* made by the local carpenter, and, putting his mouth to it, he made the serpent dance. All the village gathered round him and all the animals gathered round him, for the music of Moti Khan was blue, and the serpent danced on his tail.

When he said good-bye to his sister, he did not take the road to his concubine but went straight northwards, for Allah called him there. And at every village men came to offer food to Moti Khan and women came to offer milk to the serpent, for it swung round children's legs and swung out, and cured them of all scars and poxes and fevers. Old men slept better after its touch and women conceived on the very night they offered milk to it. Plague went and plenty came, but Moti Khan would not smell silver. That would be death.

Now sometimes, at night in caravanserais, they had wrangles.

Moti Khan used to say: 'You are not even a woman to put under oneself.'

'But so many women come to see you and so many men come to honour you, and only a king could have had such a reception though you're only a basket-maker.'

'Only a basket-maker! But I had a queen of a woman, and when she sang her voice was all flesh, and her flesh was all song. And she chewed betel-leaves and her lips were red, and even kings....'

'Stop that. Between this and the vision of the rupee....'

Moti Khan pulled at his beard and, fire in his eyes, he broke his knuckles against the earth.

'If only I could see a woman!'

'If you want God forget women, Moti Khan.'

'But I never asked for God. It is you who always bore me with God. I said I loved a woman. You are only a fanged beast. And here I am in the prime of life with a reptile to live with.'

But suddenly temple bells rang and the muezzin was heard to cry Allah-o-Akbar. No doubt it was all the serpent's work. Trembling, Moti Khan fell on his knees and bent himself in prayer.

From that day on the serpent had one eye turned to the right and one to the left when it danced. Once it looked at the men and once at the women, and suddenly it used to hiss up and slap Moti Khan's cheeks with the back of its head, for his music had fallen false and he was eyeing women. Round were their hips, he would think, and the eyelashes are black and blue, and the breasts are pointed like young mangoes, and their limbs so tremble and flow that he could sweetly melt into them.

One day, however, there was at the market a dark blue woman, with red lips, young and sprightly; and she was a butter woman. She came and stood by Moti Khan as he made the serpent dance. He played and he played on his bamboo *pungi* and music swung here and splashed there, and suddenly he looked at her and her eyes and her breasts and the *naga-swara* went and became *moha-swara*, and she felt it and he felt she felt it; and when night came, he thought and thought so much of her and she thought and thought so much of him, that he slipped to the serai door and she came to the serai gate, flower in her hair and perfume on her limbs, but lo! like the sword of God came a long, rippling light, circled round them, pinched at her nipples and flew back into the bewildering night She cried out, and the whole town waked, and Moti Khan thrust the basket under his arm and walked northwards, for Allah called him thither.

'Now,' said Moti Khan, 'I have to find God. Else this creature will kill me. And the Devil knows the hell I'd have to bake in.' So he decided that, at the next saint's tomb he encountered, he would sit down and meditate. But he wandered and he wondered; from one village he went to another, from one fair he went to another, but he found no dargah to meditate by. For God always called him northwards and northwards, and he crossed the jungles and he went up the mountains, and he came upon narrow valleys where birds screeched hereand deer frisked there but no man's voice was to be heard, and he said, 'Now let me turn back home'; but he looked back and he was afraid. And he said, 'Now I have to go to the North, for Allah calls me there.' And he climbed mountains again, and ran through jungles, and then came broad plains, and he went to the fairs and made the snake dance, and people left their rice shops and cotton-ware shops and the bellowing cattle and the yoked threshers and the querns and the kilns, and came to hear him play the music and to see the snake dance. They gave him food and fruit and cloth, but when they said, 'Here's a coin,' he said, 'Nay.' And the snake was right glad of it, for he hated to kill Moti Khan till he had found God, and he himself hated to die. Now, when Moti Khan had crossed the Narbuda and the Pervan and the Bhagirath, he came to the Jumna, and through long Agra he passed making the snake dance, and yet he could not find God and he was sore in soul with it. And the serpent was bothersome.

But at Fatehpur Sikri, he said, 'Here is Sheikh Chisti's tomb and I would rather starve and die than go one thumb-length more.' He sat by Sheikh Chisti's tomb and he said, 'Sheikh

Chisti, what is this Fate has sent me? This serpent is a very wicked thing. He just hisses and spits fire at every wink and waver. He says, "Find God." Now, tell me, Sheikh Chisti, how can I find Him? Till I find Him I will not leave this spot.'

But even as he prayed he saw snakes sprout through his head, fountains splashed and snakes fell gently to the sides like the waters by the Taj, and through them came women, soft women, dancing women, round hips, betel-chewed lips, round breasts, —shy some were, while some were only minxes—and they came from the right and went to the left, and they pulled at his beard —and, suddenly, white serpents burst through the earth and enveloped them all, but Moti Khan would not move. He said: 'Sheikh Chisti, I am in a strange world. But there is a darker world I see behind, and beyond that dark, dark world, I see a brighter world, and there, there must be Allah.'

For twenty-nine days he knelt there, his hands pressed against his ears, his face turned towards Sheikh Chisti's tomb. And people came and said, 'Wake up, old man, wake up'; but he would not answer. And when they found the snake lying on the tomb of Sheikh Chisti they cried, 'This is a strange thing', and they took to their heels; while others came and brought mullahs and maulvis but Moti Khan would not answer. For, to speak the truth, he was crossing through the dark waters, where one strains and splashes, and where the sky is all cold, and the stars all dead, and till man come to the other shore, there shall be neither peace nor God.

On the twenty-ninth night Skeikh Chisti woke from his tomb and came, his skull-cap and all, and he said: 'My son, what may I give you?'

'Peace from this serpent—and God.'

'My son, God is not to be seen. He is everywhere.'

'Eyes to see God, for I cannot any more go northwards.'

'Eyes to discern God you shall have.'

'Then peace from this serpent.'

'Faithful shall he be, true companion of the God-seeker.'

'Peace to all men and women,' said Moti Khan.

'Peace to all mankind. Further, Moti Khan, I have something to tell you; as dawn breaks Maulvi Mohammed Khan will come to offer you his daughter, fair as an oleander. She has been waiting for you and she will wed you. My blessings on you, my son !'

'Allah is found! Victory to Allah !' cried Moti Khan. The serpent flung round him, slipped between his feet and curled round his neck and danced on his head, for, when Moti Khan found God, his sins would be worn out like the quern-stone with the grindings of man, and there would be peace in all mankind.

Moti Khan married the devout daughter of Maulvi Mohammed Khan and he loved her well, and he settled down in Fatehpur Sikri and became the guardian of Sheikh Chisti's tomb. The serpent lived with him, and now and again he was taken to the fair to play for the children.

One day, however, Moti Khan's wife died and was buried in a tomb of black marble. Eleven months later Moti Khan died and he was given a white marble tomb, and a dome of the same stone, for both. Three days after that the serpent died too, and they buried him in the earth beside the dargah, and gave him a nice clay tomb. A pipal sprang up on it, and a passing brahmin planted a neem-tree by the pipal, and some merchant in the village gave money to build a platform round them. The pipal rose to the skies and covered the dome with dark, cool shade, and brahmins planted snake-stones under it, and bells rang and camphors were lit, and marriage couples went round the platform in circumambulation. When the serpent was offered the camphor Moti Khah had the incense. And when illness comes to the town, with music and flags and torches do we go, and we fall in front of the pipal-platform and we fall prostrate before the dargah, and right through the night a wind rises and blows away the foul humours of the village. And when children cry, you say, 'Moti Khan will cure you, my treasure', and they are cured. Emperors and kings have come and gone but never have they destroyed our village. For man and serpent are friends, and Moti Khan found God.

Between Agra and Fatehpur Sikri you may still find the little tomb and the pipal. Boys have written their names on the walls and dust and leaves cover the gold and blue of the pall. But someone has dug a well by the side, and if thirst takes you on the road, you can take a drink and rest under the pipal, and think deeply of God.

AN ASTROLOGER'S DAY

R. K. NARAYAN

Punctually at midday he opened his bag and spread out his professional equipment, which consisted of a dozen cowrie shells, a square piece of cloth with obscure mystic charts on it, a notebook, and a bundle of palmyra writing. His forehead was resplendent with sacred ash and vermilion, and his eyes sparkled with a sharp abnormal gleam which was really an outcome of a continual searching look for customers, but which his simple clients took to be a prophetic light and felt comforted. The power of his eyes was considerably enhanced by their position—placed as they were between the painted forehead and the dark whiskers which streamed down his cheeks: even a half-wit's eyes would sparkle in such a setting. To crown the effect he would put a saffron-coloured turban around his head. This colour scheme never failed. People were attracted to him as bees are attracted to cosmos or dahlia stalks. He sat under the boughs of a spreading tamarind tree which flanked a path running through the Town Hall Park. It was a remarkable place in many ways: a surging crowd was always moving up and down this narrow road morning till night. A variety of trades and occupations was represented all along its way: medicine sellers, sellers of stolen hardware and junk, magicians, and, above all, an auctioneer of cheap cloth, who created din all day to attract the whole town. Next to him in vociferousness came a vendor of fried groundnut, who gave his ware a fancy name each day, calling it 'Bombay Ice Cream' one day, and on the next 'Delhi Almond,' and on the third 'Raja's

Delicacy,' and so on and so forth, and people flocked to him. A considerable portion of this crowd detailed before the astrologer too. The astrologer transacted his business by the light of a flare which crackled and smoked up above the groundnut heap nearby. Half the enchantment of the place was due to the fact that it did not have benefit of municipal lighting. The place was lit up by shop lights. One or two had hissing gaslights, some had naked flares stuck on poles, some were lit up by old cycle lamps, and one or two, like the astrologer's, managed without lights of their own. It was a bewildering crisscross of light rays and moving shadows. This suited the astrologer very well, for the simple reason that he had not in the least intended to be an astrologer when he began life; and he knew no more of what was going to happen to others than he knew what was going to happen to himself next minute. He was as much a stranger to the stars as were his innocent customers. Yet he said things which pleased and astonished everyone: that was more a matter of study, practice, and shrewd guesswork. All the same, it was as much an honest man's labour as any other, and he deserved the wages he carried home at the end of a day.

He had left his village without any previous thought or plan. If he had continued there he would have carried on the work of his forefathers—namely, tilling the land, living, marrying, and ripening in his cornfield and ancestral home. But that was not to be. He had to leave home without telling anyone, and he could not rest till he left it behind a couple of hundred miles. To a villager it is a great deal, as if an ocean flowed between.

He had a working analysis of mankind's troubles: marriage, money, and the tangles of human ties. Long practice had sharpened his perception. Within five minutes he understood what was wrong. He charged three pies per question, never opened his mouth till the other had spoken for at least ten minutes, which provided him enough stuff for a dozen answers and advices. When he told the person before him, gazing at his palm, 'In many ways you are not getting the fullest results for your efforts,' nine out of ten were disposed to agree with him. Or he questioned: 'Is there any woman in your family, maybe even a distant relative who is not well disposed towards you?' Or he gave an analysis of character: 'Most of your troubles are due to your nature. How can you be otherwise with Saturn where he is? You have an impetuous nature and a rough exterior.' This endeared him to their hearts immediately, for even the mildest of us loves to think that he has a forbidding exterior.

The nuts vendur blew out his flare and rose to go home. This was a signal for the astrologer to bundle up too, since it left him in darkness except for a little shaft of green light which strayed in from somewhere and touched the ground before him. He picked up his cowrie shells and paraphernalia and was putting them back into his bag when the green shaft of light was blotted out; he looked up and saw a man standing before him. He sensed a possible client and said, 'You look so care-worn. It will do you good to sit down for a while and chat with me.' The other grumbled some reply vaguely. The astrologer pressed his invitation; whereupon the other thrust his palm under his nose, saying: 'You call yourself an astrologer?' The astrologer felt challenged and said, tilting the other's palm towards the green shaft of light: 'Yours is a nature...' 'Oh, stop that,' the other said. 'Tell me something worthwhile...'

Our friend felt piqued. 'I charge only three pies per question, and what you get ought to be good enough for your money...' At this the other withdrew his arm, took out an anna, and flung it our to him, saying: 'I have some questions to ask. If I prove you are bluffing, you must return that anna to me with interest.'

'If you find my answers satisfactory, will you give me five rupees?'

'No.'

'Or will you give me eight annas?'

'All right, provided you give me twice as much if you are wrong,' said the stranger. This pact was accepted after a little further argument. The astrologer sent up a prayer to heaven as the other lit a cheroot. The astrologer caught a glimpse of his face by the matchlight. There was a pause as cars hooted on the road, *jutka* drivers swore at their horses, and the babble of the crowd agitated the semi-darkness of the park. The other sat down, sucking his cheroot, puffing out, sat there ruthlessly. The astrologer felt very uncomfortable. 'Here, take your anna back. I am not used to such challenges. It is late for me today...' He made preparations to bundle up. The other held his wrist and said: 'You can't get out of it now. You dragged me in while I was passing.' The astrologer shivered in his grip; and his voice shook and became faint. 'Leave me today. I will speak to you tomorrow,' The other thrust his palm in his face and said: 'Challenge is challenge. Go on.' The astrologer proceeded with his throat drying up: 'There is a woman...'

'Stop,' said the other, 'I don't want all that. Shall I succeed in my present search or not? Answer this and go. Otherwise I will not let you go till you disgorge all your coins.' The astrologer muttered a few incantations and replied: 'All right. I will speak. But will you give me a rupee if what I say is convincing? Otherwise I will not open my mouth, and you may do what you like.' After a good deal of haggling the other agreed. The astrologer said: 'You were left for dead. Am I right?"

'Ah, tell me more.'

'A knife has passed through you once?' said the astrologer.

'Good fellow!' He bared his chest to show the scar. 'What else?'

'And then you were pushed into a well nearby in the field. You were left for dead.'

'I should have been dead if some passer-by had not chanced to peep into the well,' exclaimed the other, overwhelmed by enthusiasm.

'When shall I get at him?' he asked, clenching his fist.

'In the next world,' answered the astrologer. 'He died four months ago in a far-off town. You will never see any more of him.' The other groaned on hearing it. The astrologer proceeded:

'Guru Nayak—'

'You know my name !' the other said, taken aback.

'As I know all other things. Guru Nayak, listen carefully to what I have to say. Your village is two days' journey due north of this town. Take the next train and be gone. I see once again great danger to your life if you go from home.' He took out a pinch of sacred ash and held it to him. 'Rub it on your forehead and go home. Never travel southward again, and you will live to be a hundred.'

'Why should I leave home again?' the other said reflectively. 'I was only going away now and then to look for him and to choke out his life if I met him.' He shook his head regretfully. 'He has escaped my hands. I hope at least he died as he deserved.' 'Yes,' said the astrologer. 'He was crushed under a lorry.' The other looked gratified to hear it.

The place was deserted by the time the astrologer picked up his articles and put them into his bag. The green shaft was also gone, leaving the place in darkness and silence. The stranger had gone off into the night, after giving the astrologer a handful of coins.

It was nearly midnight when the astrologer reached home. His wife was waiting for him at the door and demanded an explanation. He flung the coins at her and said: 'Count them. One man gave all that.'

'Twelve and a half annas,' she said, counting. She was overjoyed. 'I can buy some jaggery and coconut tomorrow. The child has been asking for sweets for so many days now. I will prepare some nice stuff for her.'

'The swine has cheated me! He promised me a rupee,' said the astrologer. She looked up at him. 'You look worried. What is wrong?'

'Nothing.'

After dinner, sitting on the *pyol*, he told her: 'Do you know a great load is gone from me today? I thought I had the blood of a man on my hands all these years. That was the reason why I ran away from home, settled here, and married you. He is alive.'

She gasped. 'You tried to kill?'

'Yes, in our village, when I was silly youngster. We drank, gambled, and quarrelled badly one day—why think of it now? 'Time to sleep,' he said, yawning, and stretched himself on the *pyol*.

KARMA

KHUSHWANT SINGH

Sir Mohan Lal looked at himself in the mirror of a first-class waiting room at the railway station. The mirror was obviously made in India. The red oxide at its back had come off at several places and long lines of translucent glass cut across its surface. Sir Mohan smiled at the mirror with an air of pity and patronage.

The mirror smiled back at Sir Mohan.

'You are a bit of all right, old chap,' it said. 'Distinguished, efficient—even handsome. That neatly trimmed moustache—the suit from Saville Row with the carnation in the botton-hole—the aroma of eau-de-cologne, talcum powder, and scented soap all about you! Yes, old fellow, you are a bit of all right.'

Sir Mohan threw out his chest, smoothed his Balliol tie for the umpteenth time and waved a goodbye to the mirror.

He glanced at his watch. There was still time for a quick one.

'Koi hai?'

A bearer in white livery appeared through a wire-gauze door.

'Ek chota,' ordered Sir Mohan, and sank into a large cane chair to drink and ruminate.

Outside the waiting room Sir Mohan Lal's luggage lay piled along the wall. On a small grey steel trunk Lachmi, Lady Mohan Lal, sat chewing a betel leaf and fanning herself with a newspaper. She was short and fat and in her middle forties. She wore a dirty white sari with a red border. On one side of her nose glistened a diamond nose-ring and she had several gold bangles on her arms. She had been talking to the bearer until Sir Mohan had summoned him inside. As soon as he had gone, she hailed a passing railway coolie.

'Where does the zenana stop ?'

'Right at the end of the platform.'

The coolie flattened his turban to make a cushion, hoisted the steel trunk on his head, and moved down the platform. Lady Lal picked up her brass tiffin-carrier and ambled along behind him. On the way she stopped by a hawker's stall to replenish her silver betel-leaf case, and then joined the coolie. She sat down on her steel trunk (which the coolie had put down) and started talking to him.

'Are the trains very crowded on these lines ?'

'These days all trains are crowded, but you'll find room in the zenana.'

'Then I might as well get over the bother of eating.'

Lady Lal opened the brass carrier and took out a bundle of cramped chapatties and some mango pickle. While she ate, the coolie sat opposite her on his haunches, drawing lines in the gravel with his finger.

'Are you travelling alone, sister ?'

'No, I am with my master, brother. He is in the waiting room. He travels first class. He is a vizier and a barrister, and meets many officers and Englishmen in the trains—and I am only a native woman. I can't understand English and don't know their ways, so I keep to my zenana inter-class.'

Lachmi chatted away merrily. She was fond of a little gossip and had no one to talk to at home. Her husband never had any time to spare for her. She lived in the upper storey of the house and he on the ground floor. He did not like her poor illiterate relatives hanging about his bungalow, so they never came. He came up to her once in a while at night and stayed for a few minutes. He just ordered her about in anglicized Hindustani, and she obeyed passively. These nocturnal visits had, however, borne no fruit.

The signal came down and the clanging of the bell announced the approaching train. Lady Lal hurriedly finished off her meal. She got up, still licking the stone of the pickled mango. She emitted a long, loud belch as she went to the public tap to rinse her mouth and hands. After washing she dried her mouth and hands with the loose end of her sari and walked back to her steel trunk, belching and thanking the gods for the favour of a filling meal.

The train steamed in. Lachmi found herself facing an almost empty inter-class zenana compartment next to the guard's van, at the tail end of the train. The rest of the train was packed. She heaved her squat, bulky frame through the door and found a seat by the window. She produced a two-anna bit from a knot in her sari and dismissed the coolie. She then opened her betel case and made herself two betel leaves charged with a red and white paste, minced betelnuts and cardamoms. These she thrust into her mouth till her cheeks bulged on both sides. Then she rested her chin on her hands and sat gazing idly at the jostling crowd on the platform.

The arrival of the train did not disturb Sir Mohan Lal's sang-froid. He continued to sip his Scotch and ordered the bearer to tell him when he had moved the luggage to a first-class compartment. Excitement, bustle, and hurry were exhibitions of bad breeding, and Sir Mohan was eminently well bred. He wanted everything 'tickety-boo' and orderly. In his five years abroad, Sir Mohan had acquired the manners and attitudes of the upper classes. He rarely spoke Hindustani. When he did, it was like an Englishman's—only the very necessary words and properly anglicized. But he fancied his English, finished and refined at no less a place than the University of Oxford. He was fond of conversation, and like a cultured Englishman he could talk on almost any subject—books, politics, people. How frequently had he heard English people say that he spoke like an Englishman !

Sir Mohan wondered if he would be travelling alone. It was a Cantonment and some English officers might be on the train. His heart warmed at the prospect of an impressive conversation. He never showed any sign of eagerness to talk to the English as most Indians did. Nor was he loud, aggressive, and opinionated like them. He went about his business with an expressionless matter-of-factness. He would retire to his corner by the window and get out a copy of *The Times*. He would fold it in a way in which the name of the paper was visible to others while he did the crossword puzzle. *The Times* always attracted attention. Someone would like to borrow it when he put it aside with a gesture signifying, 'I've finished with it.' Perhaps someone would recognize his Balliol tie which he always wore while travelling. That would open a vista leading to a fairyland of Oxford colleges, masters, dons, tutors, boat races, and rugger matches. If both *The Times* and the tie failed, Sir Mohan would 'Koi hai' his bearer to get the Scotch out. Whisky never failed with Englishmen. Then followed Sir Mohan's handsome gold cigarette case filled with English cigarettes. English cigarettes in India ? How on earth did he get them ? Sure, he didn't mind ? And Sir Mohan's understanding smile—of course he didn't. But could he use the Englishman as a medium to commune with his dear old England ? Those five years of grey bags and gowns, of sports blazers and mixed doubles, of dinners at the Inns of Court and nights with Piccadilly prostitutes. Five years of a crowded glorious life. Worth far more than the forty-five in India with his dirty, vulgar countrymen, with sordid details of the road to success, of nocturnal visits to the upper storey and all-too-brief sexual acts with obese old Lachmi, smelling of sweat and raw-onions.

Sir Mohan's thoughts were disturbed by the bearer announcing the installation of the Sahib's luggage in a first-class coupé next to the engine. Sir Mohan walked to his coupé with a studied gait. He was dismayed. The compartment was empty. With a sigh he sat down in a corner and opened the copy of *The Times* he had read several times before.

Sir Mohan looked out of the window down the crowded platform. His face lit up as he saw two English soldiers trudging along, looking in all the compartments for room. They had their haversacks slung behind their backs and walked unsteadily. Sir Mohan decided to welcome them, even though they were entitled to travel only second class. He would speak to the guard.

One of the soldiers came up to the last compartment and stuck his face through the window. He surveyed the compartment and noticed the unoccupied berth.

"Ere, Bill,' he shouted, 'one 'ere.

His campanion came up, also looked in, and looked at Sir Mohan.

'Get the nigger out,' he muttered to his companion.

They opened the door, and turned to the half-smiling, half-protesting Sir Mahan.

'Reserved !' yelled Bill.

'Janata—Reserved. Army—Fauj,' exclaimed Jim, pointing to his khaki shirt.

'Ek dum jao—get out !'

'I say, I say, surely,' protested Sir Mohan in his Oxford accent.

The soldiers paused. It almost sounded like English, but they knew better than to trust their inebriated ears. The engine whistled and the guard waved his green flag.

They picked up Sir Mohan's suitcase and flung it into the platform. The followed his thermos-flask, suitcase, bedding, and *The Times*. Sir Mohan was livid with rage.

'Preposterous, preposterous,' he shouted hoarse with anger. 'I'll have you arrested—guard, guard !'

Bill and Jim paused again. It did sound like English, but it was too much of the King's for them.

'Keep yer ruddy mouth shut !' And Jim struck Sir Mohan flat on the face.

The engine gave another short whistle and the train began to move. The soldiers caught Sir Mohan by the arms and flung him out of the train. He reeled backwards, tripped on his bedding, and landed on the suitcase.

'Toodle-oo!'

Sir Mohan's feet were glued to the earth and he lost his speech. He stared at the lighted windows of the train going past him in quickening tempo. The tail end of the train appeared with a red light and the guard standing in the open doorway with the flags in his hands.

In the inter-class zenana compartment was Lachmi, fair and fat, on whose nose the diamond nose-ring glistened against the station lights. Her mouth was bloated with betel saliva which she had been storing up to spit as soon as the train had cleared the station. As the train sped past the lighted part of the platform, Lady Lal spat and sent a jet of red dribble flying across like a dart.

GLORY OF TWILIGHT

Bhabani Bhattacharya

The slow, narrow-gauge Indian train with its awkward freak of an engine had a way of making unauthorised stops for no good reason, between fields of corn or at the foot of a village—it was said that the guard signalled a halt to pluck a pumpkin or ripe melon from its stem or to buy fistfuls of green gram from a peasant. Some of the passengers grumbled and sat with drawn brows composing in their minds angry letters to Authority or to the Press, but others seized the chance to slip merrily out of doors for a breath of air and a view of the green fields—or a more private pursuit.

Satyajit, languid on the cushioned bench now vacated by the other occupants, reached out for his cigarettes, but on second thought withdrew his hand brusquely. That won't do, he told himself with a stern shake of his head. His smoke was rationed. He had attuned himself in the past month to a fast-growing list of denials, large and small, and this was one. How could he afford the unrestricted luxury of chain hard economy, sharpening to realities that still had the semblance of an undreamable dream.

He winced, the turning wheel of fortune in his unhappy eye, as always. Along the orbit of reminiscence he went round and round, pulled by a force beyond his will. The banking establishment of which he had attained control. The amazing tempo of it all. Luck had come his way, undeniably, but behind it was his mind, his initiative, grit, energy. Starting as a mere clerk he had become Managing Director. And now ? What now ?

Tall, thin, near forty, he had sharp features, the hair receding on his temple in wide shiny smooth patches. His eyes hated glare and he wore smart eye-glasses to shield them. His mouth, thin-lipped, would tighten in repose to a line that suggested strength of will but might have been only pride.

'What now?' he said to himself in an under-breath. Those words had become his obsession. 'What now?'

He had no business to be on this wretched train on a neglected railroad, travelling away from the city where he must look for work, for the means of living. With the sudden collapse of his bank, all his private assets were gone overnight: the equities, the house on Tagore Street; even the two cars, his and his wife's. A mercy that she was away from the scene, with her parents at Delhi, and unaware of the full extent of his ruin. A telegram had come last Tuesday announcing the safe birth of her child. Their first-born, for he had married late in life. His son, his heir. And he had sold off his diamond ring to send his young wife a remittance for the name-giving rites.

She had married a man of fortune—that made it harder for him in this crisis. True, she knew all about his earlier life. But that was story-book stuff. It could be narrated happily to their first-born when he grew older. The story lay killed by its sequel, failure. Glory was all overlaid with dark shame. Glory was dead.

It would be easy today if there were none else to think of except himself. Born in a humble village home, self-educated, struggle had been his life-breath. How grateful he was for the clerkship he secured. A turning of the wheel of fortune?—he had wondered. The next turning, a year after, was more dramatic. What made him give a fixed look to the man beyond the brass grille of the counter? The cheque presented for encashment was not a large sum. Eye upon eye. Alarm vivid in the face and the hand on the counter shaking curiously. Surprised, stirred by a quick impulse, he took the cheque to the accounts desk, compared the signature with the one on record. It tallied. But that face, that hand. A hundred reasons, none connected with the cheque, could explain the face and hand. Even so, the impulse led him to the telephone, 'Sir, have you signed a bearer cheque for Rs. 2,000? It has yesterday's date—' 'Rs. 2,000? No.' His heart felt pain for lack of air. 'Sir, are you sure? The signature seems okay.' In the next instant he was back to his counter in a rush. Where was the man? There, close to the exit, and the face turning back for a moment wore stark fear. He was going away.

Feet bounded up the counter. The bank clerk hunted down his prey on the gravel path, twenty paces from the front door. There was no struggle. The man crumpled down in a heap. He squatted with head between his hands, looking down, tears rolling down. 'Why did you have to commit forgery?' 'She has T.B.' 'She?' 'She is dying for want of medicine.' 'Who?' 'My wife. I saw no other means. I give lessons in Maths to the rich man's son. That money—' The head between the hands wagged from side to side in a queer rhythmic frenzy.

That was the way the clerk grew into an accountant. He deserved what he had gained. He was not made to be a mere clerk. Lost in the thrill, he had honest contempt for his stepping-stone, the forger. You could not commit such a crime even to save your dying wife. But today, as he sat on his lone bench on the train, he saw mindpictures and felt troubled. The crouched figure on the gravel path wrapped in mute grieving. The prisoner at the bar, face frozen, as though he had died within himself. Had he anything to say to the Court?—the Judge had asked. 'Punish me.' 'Is that all?' 'Punish me as a killer.' 'Killer?' 'I have put my wife to shame. Shame kills as fast as T.B.'

Yes, that wretched one had turned the wheel for him with his trembling hand. From that point the wheel attained a volition of its own, moving continuously. He had every reason to be grateful to the forger. Too late now to seek him out, give him a chance to live?

Too late. He himself sorely needed a chance to live. The banking business lay around him in a broken mass and there was he, prostrate on his face in the wreckage, sucking its dust. All his fault. He had tried to overreach himself. Each wrong step was now clear in time's perspective. The run on the bank had come all too suddenly though. Failure had a tempo far faster than success.

He had great need to fly from himself—that was why he was on this train. A letter had come at the nick of time offering him an excuse, a temporary relief from the wrenching within:

'The wedding of my fifth daughter, Beena, is to take place on the 20th of this month. I have kept you posted with the progress of negotiations. I seek your benediction as in the case of second, third and fourth daughters—Kamini, Damini and Suhashi. With Beena wedded, there will be only Aruna left, and she is in her tenth year. Your benediction alone can pull me through the present daughter crisis. That is all I have to say. Your helpless Uncle Srinath:'

Daughter crisis, indeed; mused Satyajit with a dim smile. Uncle Srinath, a neighbour at Shantipur village but no blood relation, seemed to have been producing his numerous daughters secure in the faith that others would bear the brunt of the repeated crises of their marriage needs. And Satyajit, in the flush of prosperity, had been more than open-handed. It was a matter of pride, self-satisfaction.

In his younger days, the village people had not thought much of him, had not seen in him any special gift or brilliance. One of the common herd. That was all the more reason why he enjoyed success. He needed the wide-eyed wonder and eager homage of Uncle Srinath and the like, while they had use and longing for his money. It was plain give-and-take.

All that was over. Fallen from his castle in the clouds, Satyajit must tread the earthly ways of humble folk. But he could not deny the old man altogether. He must send some help. He had pondered over the amount. He had to ponder over each rupee before he spent it.

Then all at once he had come to a decision. He would go to Shantipur and attend the marriage. This would be a welcome relief—the city was suffocating him. His mind would be freshened, his strength renewed for the coming struggle, by a return to the physical scene which had been his starting point in life. Let that be his starting point once more, outwardly as much as in the spirit. He would also take this chance to look at his ancestral house and fish-pond, both leased out, bits of property still intact amid the vast demolition. Those he must pass on to his wife as his last gift. And he had sent word to Uncle Srinath about his arrival on the marriage day.

The engine came to life with a shrill of warning. The passengers hurried back. Another half-hour, and it was Shantipur. Satyajit leaned out of the door, his eyes looking for Uncle Srinath on the station platform, where many people stood crowded together, alert and apparently excited, one of them holding aloft the national flag on a bamboo pole. A political celebrity on the train? Strange that Uncle Srinath, who had always feared politics, was leading the group. Suddenly there was a rush of legs towards Satyajit as he stepped down. The legs stopped and a booming chorus followed, 'Swagatam ! Welcome !'

A small girl with an awestruck face stepped up with a jasmine garland in her hand. Satyajit stood in a daze of bewilderment as the girl rose on tiptoe to place the chain of flowers around his neck. He bent mechanically to receive the offer, not knowing what it meant. It was obviously a mistake, a very curious one.

'Welcome !' the voices rang again. Then, an expectant hush.

Uncle Srinath turned round to the group. On the high cheekbones and grey stubble of his face was a clear coating of strong elation.

'Friends and brothers! Bengal has seen greatness in almost every field of action. I shall not belittle your knowledge by citing names. It is only in trade and industry that Bengal has lagged behind sadly—the plums of business have gone to people from upcountry or from overseas. That is why our hearts grow big with pride at sight of a son of our own Shantipur village, who has attained great success in that field, that forbidden field, and become the glory of the motherland. Swagatam ! Welcome !'

'Swagatam !' the combined voices roared while the tricolour flag on its tall pole nodded approvingly.

When Satyajit slipped down from the ox cart at the door of a mud-brick house, a knot of women waiting tensely with brass water-bowls rushed up and stooped over his feet, scrambling for the privilege to wash his feet with cool water. Satyajit shrank back, embarrassed.

'It's my Beena's privilege,' cried Srinath, smiling. 'This is her day. Let Beena alone wash and wipe the reverent feet. All her life she will remember this honour befalling her on the auspicious day of her marriage.'

Satyajit looked at the girl who stepped forward, shy, slender with large pensive eyes in a graceful face. 'So this is the bride,' he smiled at her and touched her hair in the gesture of blessing. 'I hope the groom is worthy of this girl,' he said as she knelt down to unlace his shoes. She slipped off his socks and poured cool water to freshen his feet, washing them with keen care. As her slim fingers went between his toes, he wiggled them, for he felt ticklish. Presently he sat on a carpet in the inner verandah with a plateful of sweets and a glass of whey, while Kamini,

Damini and Suhashi sat near him on their haunches and waved palm-leaf fans with all their energy, as though each passing minute had to be fully used before their hands were deprived of the privilege. Sweat broke out on their faces and they shifted their fans from right hand to left and again to the right. Their mother who stood by now spoke in a murmur, husky with emotion.

'You have been more of a father to these girls than he,' jerking her head at her invisible husband. 'But for the bigness of your heart, they would still be maids under this roof, shooting up in years and in height with no chance of having husband and home.' She lifted her sari fringes to her eyes, wiping off grateful tears.

The meal over, Uncle Srinath, who had been shuttling between the inner verandah and the outer quarters, now stopped, leaning over his guest.

'Beena has been given the old jewellery of her mother,' he confided. 'So, that part of the dowry problem has been met. Her three married sisters, whom you see before you and who owe all their bliss in life to your benediction, have given her the marriage gifts she must have: sari, jacket, chemise. Also brass utensils for her new household.'

'Good ! Good !' Satyajit cried happily, He had Rs. 200 in his purse and had wondered how much of it had to go into the marriage pool. May be Rs. 100; or, rather, Rs. 101, since a figure ending with zero was not propitious. During the meal he had been slowly adding to that figure: ten, twenty, finally stopping at an additional fifty. Now that Beena had got all she needed, he could just as well slice a goodly bit off the amount. Let it be Rs. 101. The fifty rupees saved would buy a perambulator for his newborn son.

'Your benediction is our blind-man's-staff,' Srinath went on. 'Do I have to say more?' He apparently decided that he did not, for he changed the topic abruptly. 'My house has become a place of pilgrimage. You are the pride of the village, its strength. In you the people see their own inmost dream fulfilled. Will you not show yourself for a minute to the devotees who sit waiting—'

Satyajit followed his host. His devotees were seated on a floor mat, talking animatedly, and at sight of him there was an instant hush. Hands joined to his chest, Satyajit made salutation to all. He caught sight of the school-master who had taught him as a boy and made a deep obeisance. Swelled with pride, the old man swept the floor mat group with a superior glance before he spoke:

'Didn't I say? Didn't I say a hundred and one times in those far-off days that the light of genius blazed on the face of my young pupil? That he stood apart from every other young pig—' He broke short and yielded to a violent fit of coughing to cover up the slip. Presently he resumed: 'That he with the light of genius on his face was afar from the world where the other youngsters dwelt? Why, I predicted that he would be a High Court Judge—'

Satyajit burst into a laugh. 'Alas, I am no High Court Judge.'

'Even more, much more !' countered the old man. His good memory reached back to the boy with whom he had been on terms of a perpetual feud. Always bent on some kind of mischief—he did have an inventive mind that way ! Arithmetic, his bogey. How does he count all his pile of money? He owns a million, if Srinath is to be believed. A million? And the old man hastened to add a brashful of colour to the drab picture presented by memory, 'Even in those far-off days I could see two shadow forms about him, clear as life—Saraswati at his left, Lakshmi at his right. And I knew even then that the twin goddesses of knowledge and of wealth, though hating the sight of each other, had for once united, stayed together, drawn by their common love.' He lifted joined palms to his forehead, offering salutation—perhaps to those goddesses.

Satyajit was determined to enjoy himself. He felt a twinge of regret that he had not thought of coming to Shantipur and basking in the people's homage when it was truly his due. Now he was an impostor. He impersonated the man he had been a few weeks before, he made an angry jerk of his hand about his face, waving off a sand-fly—and the regret. Let him be happy for the day even with a false echo, let him be wrapped awhile in the lingering twilight splendour of departed glory. Tomorrow he would be in the full fury of a stream, tugged under-water, fighting for life. Today he would have his last breath of peace, freedom, content.

Through the rest of the day he went round the village, meeting the elders, sipping the proffered milk of green coconuts. He visited his house occupied by a tenant. His house—and he touched the walls possessively. This small house gave him a feeling of security which had not come to him even from his huge city mansion. He spent an hour by the fishpond. His pond—and he sprinkled a palmful of its water on his head. A good sized carp landed at the end of his hook. When he came home with the catch, Uncle Srinath gazed at it raptly—one would have thought he had never before seen such fish. 'What gills,' he breathed in apparent ecstasy. He patted the head of the fish with an affectionate hand. 'Bride and groom shall eat curried portions of this auspicious one when they break their marriage fast at midnight. That will bring them all the blessings that life can give.'

It was near twilight when the groom's party arrived in ox carts and palanquins. Conches blew welcome. Young women gathered at the dooryard and gave the shrill traditional greeting expressive of great joy; Ulu-ulu-ulu-ulu-ulu ! When the bridal party was well settled, chewing betel leaf and waiting for the marriage hour as prescribed by the almanac, Satyajit felt for his purse. Time now to part with Rs. 101. Srinath, reading his thought, took him to the secluded darkness under a fig-tree in the backyard 'My begging bowl is ready,' he announced happily.

'Yes, yes,' Satyajit nodded.

'The cash dowry stands fixed. Only Rs. 2001.'

'What !' Satyajit felt a hard blow in the pit of his stomach.

'That is all.'

'Rs. 2,001?'

Srinath smiled. 'Everything else is provided for, even the cost of the marriage feast. Only this last item awaits your benediction.'

Benediction—Srinath's favourite word. Nothing abstract in its meaning. It could be interpreted only in terms of money. Satyajit felt a burning inside him. He had stretched his leg right into the snare of benediction, unthinkingly. How could he be so very stupid?

Srinath broke the silence with a half laugh. 'This drop in the ocean of your fortune. It shames me to mention the petty figure.'

'Why didn't you write and tell me?' The voice was harsh.

The half laugh repeated itself. 'Have I no sense? I am not such a big ass as I look. What ! Mention money to a millionaire ! And such a pittance. A drop in the ocean.'

'A drop,' echoed Satyajit, his mouth dry. This was the moment for confession. He was even wrose off than Srinath. Hard struggle lay ahead of him for bare survival. Srinath would understand.

'Millionaire !' Rhapsody in the voice. Plain worship on the face. A devotee, prayerful before his god. 'We bask in your benediction. Our life-spark itself is held in your fist; you can destroy it just by closing your fingers tight. Words cannot say what I feel—'

Yes, the god had been a millionaire, truly. That was yesterday. Today...Confession stuck in his throat, clutched by the millionaire's dead hand. Better give an excuse. He had come rushing in the midst of heavy work and had not thought of equipping himself with adequate cash. That would sound plausible. Later, it wouldn't matter if Srinath discovered the terrible truth later, as he must.

Something stronger than he spoke with his tongue. 'I had to catch the morning train—there was no time to go to the bank. May be someone in the village—' The words 'cash a cheque' were almost on his lips. 'Someone in the village will advance a loan—'

Uncle Srinath rushed out of the house, panic in his face. He had been under the impression that a millionaire always had his pockets stuffed with money. Satyajit returned to the assembled guests. Instantly the groom in his foot-high satin-draped platform, sat round cushions on three sides of him, was forgotten. Silence. All eyes took their fill of the rich man. A god on the pedestal of fortune. He too sat quiet, the tiredness within him heavier than even before. The peace he had attained erstwhile was gone. He longed to be back in town. He longed for the company of his wife. He longed to see the face of his new-born son. The rich man's son who would never ride in a perambulator.

Srinath returned in half an hour. His face looked angry. Satyajit saw his beckoning hand, rose heavily to his feet and stepped outside, away from the people.

'Only one person in Shantipur can produce so much cash at this late hour,' said Srinath. 'Harish, the money-lender. That shark refuses to make an advance though.'

The swift flood of relief! 'Harish does not trust me?' Money-lenders did have a sixth sense. There was no knowing when Harish would have got his money back—perhaps never.

'Preposterous ! Not to trust the word and signature of a millionaire ! Harish is off his senses; or, is it malice?' The voice collected anger. 'I could slap the fellow hard, slap him on each cheek. I could drag him to you and make him grovel at your feet and rub his fat nose on the ground.'

Satyajit could be generous. 'No need, no need. Trust is out of date in these cynical times.' The wonder of it—his leg was off the snare of benediction !

'Where will our India be if such things are tolerated? What is Nehru doing about it? Is there no one to tell him how things stand in the country?'

Satyajit patted the excited man on the shoulder, soothingly. Srinath controlled himself with visible effort. His face saddened. 'What is to be done?' he moaned. 'The groom's father is a man of stone. He will break off the marriage unless cash is paid to him before the ceremony starts. Who will ever marry Beena after such dishonour?'

Satyajit wagged his head in befitting sympathy. 'If only you had written to me. Just two words or three. Anyway, do not be worried. You will find another suitable match, a better one may be. Who can foresee the ways of destiny?' He felt for his purse the second time. He ought to restore the fifty rupees he had cut. Let it be Rs. 151. Even if there would be no perambulator for his son—

Srinath cleared his throat twice. 'It shames me to tell you the full story.'

'Yes?'

'Harish is willing to pay.'

'What! You have just said—'

'He will pay against security. He wants security, that evil-eyed shark. Your house and fish-pond. The madness ! To think that house and pond have more weight than a millionaire's signature !'

Satyajit trembled with him. 'House and pond,' he murmured to himself. The only possessions that had not toppled into the deluge. They were all he could give to his wife—

'All the old values destroyed, where will our India be? Has Nehru no sense to understand this? What! A pond weighs more than a millionaire's word, a house is better security than the signature of his hand! Yet, what else is to be done?' Palms folded together made supplication. 'What else is to be done in this daughter crisis?'

Satyajit had a queer drugged look. And the dead voice of the millionaire came from his throat, 'Let the money-lender pay on these terms.'

'The insult, what about the insult?' Srinath's wrathful hand cleaved the air. 'When the thing is done, I will make the shark rub his fat nose on the ground at your feet: I will do that, be sure. You will also see the whole village spit at the shark, thoo, thoo!'

The deed was signed, the house was gay with marriage music. Satyajit walked off to the deep dark under the fig tree, all by himself.

'What now?' he said under his breath, and a dim smile pinched the corners of his lips as he stuck between them the cork tip of a cigarette, the last one in the tin, and lifted a lit match with slow tremulous deliberation.

SPARROWS

KHWAJA AHMAD ABBAS

The sun was setting behind the mango grove which fringed the western extremity of the village when Rahim Khan returned from the fields. Broad and strong despite his fifty odd years, with the plough on his shoulders, and driving his two oxen, he walked through the main street of the village with a haughty and a unfriendly air. As he approached the *chaupal* where a dozen or so peasants were collected for their evening smoke, the hilarious tones of gossip died down to cautious whispers. It was only when he had vanished round the corner and the heavy tread of his footsteps was heard no more that Kallu, passing the communal *hookah* to another, remarked, 'There goes the hard-hearted devil!' To which Nanha, the fat sweet-seller, added: 'He is getting worse and worse every day. Only yesterday he beat poor Ramoo's child for throwing a pebble at his oxen.' Ramnath, the officious zaildar, volunteered further details of Rahim Khan's recent cruelties. 'And the other day he very nearly killed my mare for straying into his field.' The zaildar, of course, thought it quite irrelevant to mention that the straying of his mare had been specially planned by his own mischievous sons. The old grey-haired patel was, as usual, the last to open his toothless mouth. And as usual, his words were prefaced by a pious invocation to the Almighty. 'Hari Ram! Hari Ram!' he muttered, 'I have never seen such a cruel man. He has compassion neither for the child nor for the helpless animal. No wonder his own sons have run away from home.'

The subject of their conversation, meanwhile, had reached

his hut which, almost symbolically, stood gaunt and aloof, at a distance from the neighbouring cluster of houses. Leaning the plough up against the low wall of his house, he proceeded to tie the oxen to a pair of big wooden stakes embedded in the ground just in front of the doorway.

'Bhai Rahim Khan !' an obsequious voice said behind him as he was about to enter the house.

'What is it?' he gruffly queried, turning round to address the old woman who had come out of the house nearest his own. As she hesitated to speak he fired a volley of questions: 'What is it? I won't eat you. Why don't you speak, woman? Has your son been arrested again for revenue arrears or has your daughter-in-law delivered another baby?'

As he stopped for breath, the woman summoned up all her courage to utter two words, 'Your wife...' '...has run away.' He campleted the sentence with a grin, which broadened with the realization that he had guessed right.

'No, no,' the woman hastily explained with an apologetic look, as if she herself were responsible for his wife's absence. 'She has only gone to her brother at Nupur and will be back in a few days.'

'Bah!' he flung back at her, opening the door. He knew that his wife would never come back.

Seething with inward wrath he entered the dark hut and sat down on the charpoy. A cat mewed in a corner. Finding no one else on whom to vent his anger he flung it out, slamming the door with violence.

There was no one to give him water to wash his dust-laden feet and hands, no one to give him supper, no one whom he could curse and beat. Rahim Khan felt uncomfortable and unhappy. He had always been angry with his wife when she was there, but her absence angered him still more.

'So she's gone', he mused, lying down on the cot having decided to go to sleep without his food. During the thirty years of their married life he had always felt that she would leave him one day and, at one time he had even hoped she would. Six years ago, his eldest son Bundu had run away from home because of a more than usually severe beating. Three years later, the younger one, Nuru, joined his brother. Since that day, Rahim Khan felt sure his wife too would run away to her brother's house. But now that she had gone, he felt unhappy—not sorry, no, for he had never loved his wife—but only uncomfortable, as if a necessary piece of furniture had been removed. With her gone, on whom could he shower the outpourings of an embittered heart?

For thirty years his wife had been both the symbol and target of all his grievances against family, against society, against life.

As a youth there had been none in the village to beat him in feats of athletic skill—in wrestling, in kabadi, in diving from the canal bridge. He had loved a girl, and had wanted to join a touring circus which happened to pass through the village. In the circus, he had felt, lay the key to his ambitions—a career after his own heart—travel—fame. And in Radha, the daughter of Ram Charan, the village banya, he thought he had found his soul-mate. He had first noticed her watching him at a wrestling match and it had been the greatest moment of his life when, standing up after vanquishing his adversary, he had found Radha looking at him with the light of love in her eyes. After that there had been a few brief and furtive meetings when the unlettered but romanic youth had declared his love in passionate though halting words. But his parents had killed both ambitions. Circus work was too lowly and immoral for a respectable peasant. Anyway, his father, grandfather and all his ancestors had tilled the land, so he too had to do it. As for marrying Radha, a Hindu, a Kafir, the very idea was infamous and irreligious.

For some time, Rahim Khan, with youthful resentment, toyed with the idea of open rebellion. But the tradition of centuries of serfdom ran in his blood and, however indignant he might have felt at his father's severity, he could not summon enough courage to defy paternal authority and social traditions. After a few days, the circus left the village without Rahim Khan, and the furtive romance, with Radha too came to an abrupt end. Rahim's father slyly suggested to Ram Charan that his daughter was now fifteen and ought to have been married long ago, not failing to hint at the disastrous consequences of late marriages. Within a few weeks Radha was married to Ram Lal, a middle-aged, pot-bellied banya of the neighbouring village. With a few sad tears shed in the solitude of the night in memory of her hopeless romance with Rahim Khan, she quickly reconciled herself to her fate and proceeded forthwith to be the mother of half-a-dozen children.

Rahim Khan also married. He had, of course, no choice in the matter. His parents selected the girl, fixed the date, ordered some gaudy clothes for him and some silver ornaments for his bride, sat him on a horse and, to the beat of a brass band, took him to the girl's house where the Nikah was duly performed. To the Kazi's formal questions Rahim Khan mechanically nodded his head. Any other course was impossible. Nobody, of course, cared to ask the shy little girl who sat huddled in a dark room only dimly conscious of the fate to which she had been condemned. After the ceremony, Rahim Khan's father, in a mood of self-congratulation, boasted to his wife: 'See how meekly he obeyed me. You always feared he might refuse to fall in with our arrangements. I know these youngsters. They are apt to be restless if their marriage is delayed. That is why our fathers believed in marrying away their children early. Now he will be all right!'

At that very moment, standing on the threshold of the room where his wife awaited him much as a sheep awaits the butcher,

Rahim Khan made a terrible resolve to avenge himself on his parents, his family, on society. He held them all responsible for the frustration of his life's dreams. And in his confused, illogical mind he regarded his bride as the symbol of the persecution to which he had been subjected. On her he would wreak his vengeance. Iron entered his hitherto kindly soul as he rudely pushed open the door.

That was thirty years ago. Rahim Khan reflected as he lay there on his cot in the dark hut. And hadn't he had his revenge? For thirty years he had ill-treated his wife, his children and his bullocks, quarrelled with everyone in the village and made himself the most hated person in the whole community. The thought of being so universally detested gave him grim satisfaction.

No one in the village, of course, understood or tried to understand the reasons for this strange transformation of the cheerful and kind young man into the beast that he had become. At first, their attitude towards him was one of astonished hostility, but later it changed to indifference mingled with fear. Of understanding and sympathy he received none. Shunned by everyone, with a bitterness ever gnawing at his heart, Rahim Khan sought consolation in the unquestioned authority over his wife which society allowed him.

For thirty years his wife had submitted to his persecution with the slave-like docility that is the badge of her tribe. Lately, indeed, she had become so used to corporal chastisement that it seemed unnatural if a whole week passed without a beating. To Rahim Khan beating his wife had become a part of his very existence. As sleep gathered round him, his last thought was whether he would be able to endure a life without having an opportunity of indulging in what had now become his second nature. It was perhaps the only moment when Rahim Khan had a feeling, not exactly of affection, for his wife, but of loneliness without her. Never before had he realized how much the woman he hated was a part of his life.

When he awoke it was already late forenoon and he started the day by cursing his wife, for it was she who used to wake him early every morning. But he was in no great hurry today. Lazily he got up and, after his ablutions, milked the goats for his breakfast which consisted of the remains of the previous day's chapattis soaked in the fresh milk. Then he sat down for a smoke, with his beloved *hookah* beside him. Now the hut was warm and alight with the rays of the sun streaming in through the open window. In a corner they revealed some cobwebs and, having already decided to absent himself from his fields, he thought he would tidy his hut. Tying some rags to the end of the long pole, he was about to remove the cobwebs when he saw a nest in the thatched roof. Two sparrows were fluttering in and out, twittering constantly.

His first impulse was to wreck the nest with one stroke of his pole, but something within him made him desist. Throwing down the pole, he brought a stool and climbed up on it to get a better view of the sparrows' home. Two little featherless mites of red flesh, baby sparrows hardly a day old, lay inside, while their parents hovered round Rahim Khan's face, screaming threateningly. He barely had a glimpse of the inside of the nest when the mother sparrow attacked him.

'Oh damn, you vixen, you might have plucked out my eye,' exclaimed Rahim Khan with his characteristic hollow laugh, and climbed down from his perch. He was strangely amused by the little bird's heroic efforts to save their home and children. The sparrows' nest suffered no harm that day and peace reigned in Rahim Khan's hut.

Next day he resumed his daily work. Still no one talked to m in the village. From morning till late in the afternoon he would toil in the field, ploughing the furrow and watering the crops, but he returned home before sunset. Then he would lie on his cot, smoking his *hookah* and watching with lively interest the antics of the sparrow family. The two little ones had now grown into fine young birds, and he called them Nuru and Bundu after his lost sons whom he had not seen for several years. The four sparrows were his only friends in the world. His neighbours were still frightened of him and regarded his recent peaceful behaviour with suspicion. They were genuinely astonished that for some time no one had seen him beating his bullocks. Nathoo and Chhiddoo themselves were happy and grateful and their bruised bodies had almost healed.

One monsoon evening, when the sky was overcast with threatening clouds, Rahim Khan returned from the fields a little earlier than usual. He found a group of children playing on the road. They ran away as they saw him, and even left their shoes behind in their haste. In vain did Rahim Khan shout, 'Why are you running away ? I am not going to beat you.' Meanwhile, it had started drizzling and he hurried homewards to tie up the bullocks before the big down-pour came.

Entering his hut, Rahim Khan lighted the earthen-ware oil lamp and placed some crumbs of bread for the sparrows before he prepared his own dinner. 'O Nuru ! O Bundu !' he shouted, but the sparrows did not come out. Anxious to find out what had happened to his friends, he peered into the nest and found the quartet scared and sitting huddled up within their feathers. At the very spot where the nest lay, the roofwas leaking. Rahim Khan took a ladder and went out in the pouring rain to repair the damage. By the time the job was satisfactorily done he was thoroughly drenched. As he sat on the cot, Rahim Khan sneezed, but he did not heed the warning and went to sleep. Next morning he awoke with a high fever.

When the villagers did not see him going to the fields for several days they grew anxious and some of them came to see what was the matter. Through a crack in the door they saw him lying on the cot talking, so they thought, to himself. 'O Bundu, O Nuru, who will feed you when I am gone ?'

The peasants shook their heads sympathetically. 'Poor fellow,' they said, 'he has gone mad. We will send for his wife to look after him.'

Next morning when Rahim Khan's wife, anxious and weeping, came with her sons, a group of neighbours collected in sympathy. The door was locked from the inside, and in spite of loud knocking no one opened it. When they broke their way in they found the large and gaunt frame of Rahim lying in the brooding silence of the room, broken only by the flutterings of four sparrows.

THE FLOOD

Kamala Markandaya

Nature is like a wild animal that you have trained to work for you. So long as you are vigilant and walk warily with thought and care, so long will it give you its aid; but look away for an instant, be heedless or forgetful, and it has you by the throat.

My daughter Ira had been given in marriage in the month of June, and what with the preparing for it, and the listlessness that took hold of me in the first days after her departure, nothing was done to make our hut weatherproof or to secure the land from flooding. That year the monsoon broke early with an evil intensity such as none could remember before.

It rained so hard, so long, and so incessantly that the thought of a period of no rain provoked a mild wonder. It was as if nothing had ever been but rain, and the water pitilessly found every hole in the thatched roof to come in, dripping on to the already damp floor. If we had not built on high ground the very walls would have melted in that moisture. I brought out as many pots and pans as I had, and we laid them about to catch the drips, but soon there were more leaks than we had vessels.... Fortunately, I had laid in a stock of firewood for Ira's wedding, and the few sticks that remained served at least to cook our rice, and while the fire burnt, hissing at the water in the wood, we huddled round trying to get dry. At first the children were cheerful enough—they had not known such things before, and the lakes and small streams that formed outside gave them endless delight; but Nathan and I watched with heavy hearts while the waters rose and rose and the tender green of the paddy field sank under and was lost.

'It is a bad season,' Nathan said sombrely. 'The rains have destroyed much of our work; there will be little eating done this year.'

At these words, Arjun broke into doleful sobs and his brother, Thambi, followed suit. They were old enough to understand, but the others, who weren't, burst into tears too, for by now they were cramped and out of humour with sitting crouched on the damp floor; and hungry since there was little to eat, for most of the food had gone to make the wedding feast, and the new season's harvesting lay outside ungathered and rotting. I hushed them as best as I could, throwing a reproachful glance at my husband for his careless words, but he was unnoticing, sunk in hatred and helplessness.

As night came on—the eighth night of the monsoon—the winds increased, whining and howling ground our hut as if seeking to pluck it from the earth. Indoors it was dark—the wick, burning in its shallow saucer of oil, threw only a dim, wavering light—but outside the land glimmered, sometimes pale and sometimes vivid, in the flicker of lightning. Towards midnight the storm was at its worst. Lightning kept clawing at the sky almost continuously, thunder shook the earth. I shivered as I looked—for I could not sleep, and even a prayer come with difficulty.

'It cannot last,' Nathan said. 'The storm will go down by the morning.'

Even as he spoke, a streak of lightning threw itself down at the earth. There was a tremendous clap of thunder, and when I uncovered my shrinking eyes I saw that our coconut plant had been struck. That, too, the storm had claimed for its own.

In the morning everything was calm. Even the rain had stopped. After the fury of the night before, an unnatural stillness lay on the land. I went out to see if anything could be saved of the vegetables, but the shoots and vines were battered and broken, torn from their supports and bruised; they did not show much sign of surviving. The corn field was lost. Our paddy field lay beneath a placid lake on which the children were already sailing bits of wood.

Many of our neighbours fared much worse than we had. Several were homeless, and of a group of men who had sheltered under a tree when the storm began six had been killed by lightning.

Kali's hut had been completely destroyed in the last final fury of the storm. The roof had been blown away bodily, the mud walls had crumbled.

'At least it stood until the worst was over', said Kali to me, 'and by God's grace we were all spared.' She looked worn out; in the many years I had known her I had never seen her so deflated. She had come to ask for some palm leaves to thatch the new hut her husband was building; but I could only point to the blackened tree, its head bitten off and hanging by a few fibres from the withered stump.

'We must thatch our roof before the night,' I said. 'The rains may come again. We need rice too.'

Nathan nodded. 'We may be able to buy palm leaves in the village—also rice.'

He went to the granary, in a corner of which the small cloth bundle of our savings lay buried. It had been heavy once, when we were newly married: now the faded rag in which it tied was too big and the ends flapped loosely over the knot. Nathan untied it and counted out twelve rupees.

'One will be enough,' I said. 'Let us go.'

'I will take two. We can always put it back.'

In the village the storm had left disaster and desolation worse than on our own doorstep. Uprooted trees sprawled their branches in ghastly fashion over streets and houses, flattening then and the bodies of men and women. Sticks and stones lay scattered wildly in angry confusion. The tannery stood, its bricks and cement had held it together in spite of the raging winds; but the workers' huts, of weaker construction, had been demolished. The thatch had been ripped from some; where others stood there was now only a heap of mud with their owners' possessions stuck in them in a kind of pitiless decoration. The corrugated-iron shacks in which some of the men lived were no more: here and there were we could see the iron sheets in unexpected places—suspended from tree tops, or blown and driven into the walls of houses still left standing. There was water everywhere, the gutters were overflowing into the streets. Dead dogs, cats, and rats cluttered the road-side, or floated on the waters with blown, distended bellies.

People were moving about amid this destruction, picking out a rag here, a bundle there, hugging those things that they thought to be theirs, moving uncertainly and with a kind of despair about them. People we knew came and spoke to us in low voices, gesturing hopelessly.

'Let us go, it is no good; we'll come back later.'

We turned back, the two rupees unspent. Our children came running out to meet us, their faces bright with hope.

'The shops are closed or destroyed,' I said. 'Go inside, I will get you some gruel presently.'

Their faces faded; the two younger ones began crying listlessly from hunger and disappointment. I had no words to comfort them.

At dusk the drums of calamity began; their grave, throbbing rhythm came clearly through the night, throughout the night, each beat, each tattoo, echoing the mighty impotence of our human endeavour. I listened. I could not sleep. In the sound of the drums I understood a vast pervading doom; but in the expectant silences between, my own disaster loomed large more important, and more hurtful.

We ventured out again when the waters had subsided a little, taking with us as before two rupees. This time things were somewhat better; the streets were clear, huts were going up everywere. My spirits rose.

'To Hanuman, first for rice,' said Nathan, excited. 'The gruel we have been swallowing has been almost plain water these last few days'.

I quickened my steps; my stomach began heaving at the thought of food.

Hanuman was standing in the doorway of his shop. He shook his head when he saw us. 'You have come for rice,' he said. 'They all come for rice. I have none to sell, only enough for my wife and children.'

'And yet you are a merchant who deals in rice?'

'And what if so? Are you not growers of it? Why, then, do you come to me? If I have rice, I do not choose to sell it now; but I have told you, I have none'.

'We ask for only a little. We will pay for what we have—see, here is the money.'

'No, no rice but—wait...they say Biswas is selling...you can try....'

To Biswas. 'We come for rice. Look, here is our money.'

'Two rupees? How much do you think yon can buy with two rupees?'

'We thought——'

'Never mind what you thought! Is this not a time of scarcity? Can you buy rice anywhere else? Am I not entitled to charge more for that?'

'It is very little for two rupees——'

'Take it or leave it. I can get double that sum from the tanners, but because I know you——'

We take it, we give up the silver coins. Now there is nothing left for the thatching, unless we use a rupee or two from the ten that remain in the granary.

I put the rice in my sari, tuck the precious load securely in at the waist. We turn back. On the outskirts of the village there is Kenny. His face is grim and long, his eyes are burning in his pale face. He sees us and comes up.

'You, too, are starving, I suppose',

I tap the roll at my waist—the grains give at my touch.

'We have a little rice—it will last us untill times are better.'

'Times are better, times are better,' he shouts. 'Times will not be better for many months. Meanwhile you will suffer and die, you meek suffering fools. Why do you keep this ghastly silence? Why do you not demand—cry out for help—do something? There is nothing in this country, Oh God, there is nothing !'

We shrink from his violence. What can we do—what can he mean? The man is mad. We go on our way.

The paddy was completely destroyed; there would be no rice until the next harvesting. Meanwhile, we lived on what remained of our salted fish, roots and leaves, the fruit of the prickly pear, and on the plantains from our tree. At last the time came for the rice terraces to be drained and got ready for the next sowing. Nathan told me of it with cheer in his voice, and I told the children, pleasurably, for the fields were full of fish that would feed us for many a day. Then we waited, spirits lifting, eyes sparkling, bellies painful with anticipation.

At last the day, Nathan went to break the dams and I with him and with me our children, sunken-eyed, noisy as they had not been for many days at the thought of the feast, carrying nets and baskets. First one hole, then another, no bigger than a finger's width, until the water eroded the sides and the outlets grew large enough for two fists to go through. Against them we held our nets, feet firm in the mud while the water rushed away, and the fish came tumbling into them. When the water was all gone there they were caught in the meshes and among the paddy, shoals of them leaping madly, wet and silver and good to look upon. We gathered them with flying fingers and greedy hearts and bore them away in triumph, with a glow at least as bright as the sun on those shining scales. Then we came and gathered up what remained of the paddy and took it away to thresh and winnow.

Late that night we were still at work, cleaning the fish, hulling the rice, separating the grain from the husk. When we had done, the rice yield was meagre, no more than two measures—all that was left of the year's harvest and the year's labour.

We ate, finding it difficult to believe we did so. The good food lay rich, if uneasy, in our starved bellies. Already the children were looking better, and at the sight of their faces, still thin but content, a great weight lifted from me. Today we would eat and tomorrow, and for many weeks while the grain lasted. Then there was the fish, cleaned, dried, and salted away and before that was gone we should earn some more money; I would plant more vegetables...such dreams, delightful, orderly, satisfying, but only dreams. And sleep, such sleep ...deep and sweet and sound as I had not known for many nights; it claimed me even as sat amid the rice husks and fish scales and drying salt.

CIRCUS CAT, ALLEY CAT

ANILA DESAI

I first saw Anna, the new 'nanny' of the English children who lived next door, in a pink stucco house, late one evening when she came to hound us out of the shrubbery where we were playing hide-and-seek, a game which, as anyone knows, grows exciting only at dinner time. I crept behind a screen of bamboo and peered out at her through the polished bars of the bamboo stalks. She was large and heavily built with very black bright eyes and a lot of wiry black hair. She bent down to pick up a neem switch and slapped it against her thigh as she called to us in a loud, sharp voice. And through the cage of bamboos, in that blue twilight, I saw the lawn turn to a saw-dust covered stage floor and Nanny's white uniform into spangled pink tights and the switch in her hand to a long, whistling whip that cracked in the air which was filled no longer with the talking of mynah birds and the barks of pet dogs, but with the roars of tigers and the gibbering of apes. Sick with terror, I found I could scarcely breathe and preferred to creep over the manure pit to my own home than on to the lawn and face to face with Nanny.

My imagination was fired, no doubt, as much by the fact that I had only that morning heard that Nanny came from a circus where she had worked as cat-trainer, as by the cracking of the switch in her hand and her hefty shoulders and authoritative voice. How the staid, plain and entirely unimaginative family of Bates could choose a circus performer to be a Nanny for their children is an eternal mystery, though they endeavoured to explain it to us as an act of charity. Anna, they told us (her real name, or stage name, was Shakti—Strength ! Power!—but the Bateses preferred to call her by the more tame and domestic name of Anna) was a Malabar girl who had been born into the circus, and had trained the big cats since she was thirteen. Her special 'breath-taking, death-defying, terror-striking' act was to drape a tiger over her shoulders and stand on the backs of two lions whom she would then order to emit great, rumbling roars that made her large frame tremble all over and the tiger snarl. Dressed in parrot-green tights and a lilac shirt with silver spangles, her fierce mane of hair standing on end, she must have looked a sight. Then she married the boy who fed the cats. The boy was ambitious. In no time, he had taught her that a woman's place is her home and was straddling the lions himself and wrapping the tiger round his own neck. Anna, in a spurt of cat-like temper, left. By that time she had a baby, and when Mrs. Bates found her, she and the child were near starvation, begging on a Daryaganj street. Mrs. Bates gave her a white uniform and put bath-salts in her tub in order to wash off that special circus odour of elephant manure and cat sweat; she was installed as the children's Nanny, and her baby put in a cradle on the back verandah and fed on milk and oranges.

All this played real havoc on our imagination, as nothing had ever done before. She had only to rattle the knobs of the windows and doors as she banged them shut against the summer heat, to make us feel we were being shut into our cages. We would no longer walk, or run, but prowl. We would not hop or skip, but spring and leap. Even our voices changed. Anna had only to come into the room with a tricycle or our skipping-ropes, and we would feel the trainer had arrived, wooden chair in hand, to practise the act, and in this spirit we would play the games she ordered us to play. Anna had only to sit down at the breakfast table and cut the bread into slices for us, to make us think of it as a great hunk of fresh meat, dripping with scarlet blood, and we would shudder as we gnawed at it. A cooking-spoon in Anna's hand would become a biting, snapping, snaky whip. A plain brooch pinned to her lapel would change the plain white uniform to a gaudy, satin stage costume. When the lights were switched on at night, the brightness of Anna's eyes was the brightness of a stage-performer's eyes in the glare of white-hot oil lamps. No matter how hard Mrs. Bates tried to domesticate her and turn her into a tame alley-cat, a nice, motherly pussy-cat, Anna remained to us the 'breath-taking death-defying, terror-striking' Anna of the circus. Poor Anna herself played no part in this. No matter how hard we tried, and how cleverly, she never spoke of the circus once. Yet the very house, with its Rangoon creeper, its worn rugs and nursery pictures, became the Big Top for us, the dinnerbell, the big drums, the lights, the spot-lights of the stage. We lived in a constant quiver of thrill upon thrill! I dreamt of cats all the night, long-striped cats leaping in the air, great cats shaking their manes as they roared, their musles rippling under the smooth skin, the shining hair. They sprang soundlessly from dream to dream, landing softly on my eye-lids, and from strangers of the jungle they became companions of the long nights of excitement.

And then Anna's baby vanished. I came across Anna in the garden one day, her hair more disordered than ever, her eyes red from weeping. 'My baby's gone!, she cried theatrically. 'My baby's been taken away. Oh God, Oh God, give my baby back to me—but I'll never see her again—she's been taken away from me.' And I joined whole-heartedly in the weeping to think that God had taken the child at such a tender age and left poor Anna all alone. As I ran back to the house to tell my mother, I wondered if the baby had suddenly been taken ill, because she had seemed very healthy and well only the previous day. My mother was, for this reason, equally shocked and immediately went to see Anna.

Anna wept on her shoulders, looking quite thin and pathetic in her sorrow. My mother pressed her hand and soothed her, 'What God decrees, we must accept Anna. It is sad but it must be, Anna.' On her way out, she looked in on Mrs. Bates, and asked, 'When is the funeral to be ?'

'The funeral ?' Mrs. Bates jumped. 'What funeral ?'

'Why, of poor Anna's baby !'

'Anna's baby ? Why, is it dead ?'

We were nonplussed that the mistress of the house should not have heard of the tragedy yet. My mother and I interrupted each other in trying to tell her what had happened and were horrified when the kind old missionary's wife chortled and clapped her hand over her mouth to stop her laughter.

'The baby dead !' she cried. 'Whatever gave you the idea ? It's only that Anna's husband and his family came and took it away. We're trying to get it back, only the circus has moved to Bombay now so it will be a bit difficult. We're sending Anna off to try though'.

That was the last we saw of Anna for a long time. The next time was several years later when we went to see a circus and found Shakti's name on the handbill, and a picture of Anna with a snarling tiger on her shoulders. She was smiling hugely.

We could scarcely wait till she appeared and then were so excited we could not even applaud. We watched out for her baby and wondered if it had grown into the little girl who was somersaulting in the sawdust and tumbling around with a deeply preoccupied expression on her thin face. But throughout the performance, the thought upper-most in my mind was : where is Anna's husband ? And I had a vivid picture of Anna in a great cage, gnawing, gnawing upon a great, bleeding hunk of flesh, Anna snarling at the people who came to snatch it from her, Anna throwing back her mane and giving a great roar of triumph, Anna the queen of the circus cats, Anna the circus cat...

THE HOMECOMING

Arun Joshi

Since he returned from the war things had not been quite the same. He had fought on the Eastern Front in Dinajpur, where he was told, the fighting had been rough. Personally, he did not know. He had been commissioned only the previous year and this had been his first war. He did not quite know what was rough and what was not. It was true, though, that half his men had been killed during the two weeks. Nine had died on the very first night.

The day he returned his fiancee and his family met him at the station. They embraced, and wept, and, later on they laughed. His fiancee wore an emerald green sari and in the winter sun, he thought, she looked very pretty. She asked him if the war had been bad. He said it had been all right but he wished so many of his men had not been killed. She said she had been simply dying for him to come back. He said that was very nice of her. Then they talked of the blackouts and the air raids and things they had seen on the T.V. By the time they reached home—it was about twenty minutes drive from the station—she was saying that because of staying cooped indoors for so many evenings she had been eating too much and would now have to diet. His mother said dieting gave anaemia. Anaemia, she hinted, was bad for child-bearing.

Now, where he had come from, for days on end, he had not met a man, woman, or child, who had not been hungry; always hungry. Everyone was hungry, once in a way, but to be always hungry, he had seen, was different. It made a bit of an animal of you, he thought, turned you stupid. After the ceasefire he had supervised a relief station. People used to line up two hours in advance although there was nothing to do except sit and watch the cooks and sniff the air. When they got their ration they swallowed it in about two minutes. After that he could see they were as hungry as before, that in fact they were waiting for the next meal. The old people had not bothered to look for food. If it came their way they ate it. If not, they lay down and died. That was the way it had been where he had come from. So when his fiancee talked of dieting and with what his mother said of anaemia he started to feel a little lost.

His mother was very keen on his marriage. So was he, in a way—until before the war. During the war he had killed ten men, led assaults that ended the lives of many others and had seen several hundred dead, gashed, charred, bloated, hacked, shot through with their hands behind their backs. He had seen bodies gorging the viaducts of canals, flaking off like stale cake. Once he saw a hockey field strewn with the skeletons of boys. That was the first time he had seen dead people aside from the corpses that he had seen carried around for cremation. His family were well-to-do and there had not yet been a death. So he had not seen a dead body before and now he had seen hundreds of them. And he had been wondering about marriage. What was the meaning of one man's marriage; one man's life. He had been wondering what life was all about. Who, he had been thinking, could possibly be running the world. Such thoughts filled his head with confusion as he sat about or played cards or went out with his father for a game of golf.

He wanted to tell someone about his thoughts. He had no brothers. His father was a businessman. He thought it stupid that he should join the army when the family business was there. His father had donated a lot of soap for the soldiers. He did not make soap. He had bought it from a friend at wholesale. Now he was very busy because he thought a big boom was on the way on account of the heavy demand from the East. He was very busy and he did not have much time for his son.

He had a sister. He used to know her. Now she had changed. He couldn't put his finger on it. But she had changed. She wore strange clothes and shiny chains and goggles. She wore goggles even at night. At times she wore these for riding. She talked strangely, too.

One day she took him to a party. As a rule he didn't go to parties—they depressed him and worked on his nerves—but she said it was a party of young people. He went because he had been having these thoughts and he hoped he could talk them over with someone. May be, he thought, he would feel a little better, more at home.

It was a small party. He knew most people. They were the children of businessmen whom he had known all his life. But most of them had changed. The boys had long hair and side-burns and some had beards. A couple of girls were without bras. The others wore pant suits and chains and goggles. All except him smoked. Just before the war ended he had taken in a lot of sulphur dioxide in an artillery barrage and he had been told to keep off smoking for a while. But he could drink. And he drank. All of them talked. In fact they were quite good at it. They could build things up, one on top of another, like children's blocks. One of them said the need was to see things whole, in perspective; to conceptualize. He did not know what that meant but, he thought, it meant building things up, one upon the other. There was a long haired boy who had once been in his literature class. Now, he said, he was a poet.

The poet seemed very keen to define genocide. He also wanted everybody to accept his definition. He said it was important to define genocide because how else did one know whether genocide had taken place. He said a great many cruel things had no doubt been done, but it was not correct to say that they amounted to genocide. The things that had happend, he said, did not meet the definition of genocide. Everyone was impressed because the poet said things different from what the press and everyone else had been saying.

They talked about the war and he listened. They talked of the things they had read in newspapers and magazines. He did not know what they had read but a lot of things they said were not quite correct. They mixed up terms. Bazookas and mortars, for example, were not the same, nor was an out-flanking manoeuvre the same as a pincer. But everyone seemed keen to use big words.

They also had their own views on how a war was fought. They thought you fought from trenches and with tanks and guns and aeroplanes. They asked him what happened after the tanks and the artillery and the aeroplanes were done with the enemy. He said the enemy was usually still there after they were done. You had to go out and fight him. They didn't seem to believe him.

After dinner everyone was a little groggy. The poet said he would recite a poem.

He read out casually from the back of an envelope but his face wore the death-look. He talked of Golden Bengal bleeding under a violet sky. Everyone became very serious, goggles and all. Some of the girls looked very sad. 'But no matter,' the poet concluded, 'no matter, comrades, you shall not be forgotten, nor your death go unavenged.' He recited something like that.

The death-look still on his face, he asked him if he liked the poem. He said it was fine if that was how it seemed to him. Personally he remembered different things. He remembered, for example, pushing a boat off a bank, under the light of stars, into a pitch-black stream whose name he did not know. He remembered the silhouettes of the six boys in the boat. They had been detailed to demolish a bridge. When he pushed them off the bank he knew they would not come back. So did they. He knew they would be killed before or after the bridge was blown. Whichever way you looked at it, the boys knew, they would not come back. The oldest among them was nineteen. None of them had long hair or beards and none wore the death-look They just sat quietly, six silhouettes, a little defiant, a little afraid. He said he did not know much about violet skies but he knew it wasn't easy to die. And to die at nineteen—that, he said, was beyond his imagination.

Another time, he said, they walked into a village and there was a child stuck on a bayonet in front of every hut. There was nobody in the village; just a dead child stuck on a bayonet before every hut.

Then there was the schoolful of girls that had been the brothel for a battalion. A battalion, he told them, was a thousand men.

So, he said to the boys, if one were to write poems one would have to get it all in, all of this and much else. And he didn't know what sort of poems could get all of it in.

One day he learnt he had been awarded the Vir Chakra. It had been given to him for the night right at the start, the one in which nine of his men had been killed. He had often thought of that night.

He had been told to take an outpost. There had been a lot of shelling and machine-gun fire. Finally, he had ordered a direct assault. There was not much else he could do because they were short of time. They were short of time because beyond the outpost was a highway where a convoy had to be intercepted. He had hoped they would take the enemy by surprise. But as they got within range there was heavy fire from all sides: Brens and machine-guns and a lot of grenades. Some of them were killed at once. Finally they were in the trenches. There was a bayonet charge and the decisive fight which they had won and for which he had got the Vir Chakra. But that bayonet charge kept troubling him.

At times when you charged with a bayonet it got locked inside the man. You could do things to draw it or you could fire your weapon so that it was released with the recoil. In any case you lost some seconds.

It was quite dark in the trenches. They had not been able to keep a close formation. One of his subedars was fighting to the left of him when his bayonet stuck. A soldier moved towards him. He remembered the sheen of moonlight on the soldier's bayonet, pointing towards his belly. The Subedar saw it too and saw that he was stuck. He turned, which, in his own defence, he should not have. The Subedar tackled the soldier. The next moment he was bayonetted himself. He was one of the nine that were killed.

He had visited the Subedar's family. They lived in a mud hut in a circle of mud huts. He had met his mother. She had cried and wanted to touch his hand. Please help us, she had said. You are big people; you can help. The Subedar's widow was a little younger than his fiancee. They had two children; two years and nine months. He had recommended an award for the Subedar. His children could study free up to college. His widow would get a pension. But he didn't know what she would do. He wondered what a girl did when she got widowed at twenty and couldn't marry again.

While he was on leave things kept swirling about his head. He lay awake most nights trying to make sense out of things. At times he wished he had a bagful of grenades that, some evening he could lob, one each, in every door-way down the street; or that there were a war, not a thousand miles away, but right in the heart of their city, in their streets and parks. At other times he was afraid. Dark shapes danced before his eyes and his palms grew moist. What would he do, he wondered, if there were other wars and other bayonet charges and more boys in boats to be pushed into the silence of the night. Sometimes he thought of leaving the Army. Even so how could he be sure that he would not awake in the middle of the night and not know that somewhere a lieutenant was making a charge, that some

Subedar, with a wife and children, was getting bayonetted in the moonlight.

But in the morning there were the parties and movies and dancing and the flowers in their garden. There was his sister with her new car, the chains around her waist angling everytime she moved. There were the poets who hadn't seen a gun and arty-arty girls, and charity fetes and speeches on the radio. There was his mother insisting he marry straightway and, of course, his father getting ready for the boom. He did not know how to fit it all together or whether it could be fitted together. Ever.

NOTES

Essays

THE SECRET OF WORK

Swami Vivekanand (1863-1902) is one of the makers of modern India. His first name was Narendranath Dutt, but he became Vivekanand after he joined the Ashram of Ramkrishna Paramhans as his disciple. In his short span of life, he toured extensively in India and abroad and delivered scores of lectures in order to propagate the ideals of his teacher. He was perhaps the first Indian to raise his country and its culture in the eyes of the West. His lectures and writings possess a clarity and force which comes not only from the mastery of the language but also from his total commitment to the cause he was working for.

In 'The Secret of Work', an extract from his *Karma-yoga*, Swami Vivekanand gives a remarkable exposition of the idea of non-attachment to action.

miseries: great sufferings
pure: free from sin
charitable asylum: a free place of rest and recuperation
entail: impose
forge fetters: make chains
sojourner: one who stays for a short time
drudge: a person who works hard at unpleasant tasks

INTERNATIONALISM

Mystic, yogi, philosopher, poet and critic, Sri Aurobindo (1872—1950) is one of the tallest figures of modern India. He took a first class classical Tripos at Cambridge, and, on his return to India, worked for some time as a lecturer at Baroda. For a brief period he took active part in politics, but later he retired to Pondicherry to devote himself entirely to philosophic and religious meditation. His works include *Life Divine*, *Synthesis of Yoga*, and the epic poem *Savitri*.

idealistic stages: the times when the French revolutionaries were guided by the ideals of liberty, equality and fraternity.

anarchism: total absence of law; extreme individualism
maleficient: evil
futurist: looking forward to an ideal state in the future
effectuation: becoming effective
abjuration: renunciation
syndicalist: one who aims at the transfer of the means of production and distribution from the owners to the unions of workers
sans-patrie: without a native land

INDIAN CIVILIZATION AND CULTURE

M.K. Gandhi (1869-1948), hailed as the father of the Indian nation, was more a spiritual leader than a politician. After studying Law in London, he went to South Africa where he started the Civil Disobedience Movement. Later, he led the struggle for the independence of India, and successfully made use of the two great weapons of truth and non-violence.

His autobiography, *My Experiments with Truth*, and the numerous articles that he wrote for *Young India* and the speeches that he delivered on different occasions, reveal him not only as an original thinker but also as a great master of chaste, idiomatic English.

Pharaos: rulers of ancient Egypt

sheet-anchor: security
life-corroding: destroying life gradually
touts: persons employed in soliciting customers
votaries: devotees
Gibbon: the English historian of the eighteenth century who authored the famous book *The Decline and Fall of the Roman Empire.*
Golden Fleece: an object very difficult to attain. The Golden Fleece of Greek mythology was well-protected by snakes and flames, and to secure it Jason had to employ the magic of Media.

EDUCATION FOR NEW INDIA

Chakravarti Rajgopalachari (1879-1972) was a brilliant lawyer, statesman and scholar and a forceful speaker and writer. He gave up his fabulous practice as a lawyer to join the Congress and the national movement for freedom, but formed his own political party, the Swatantra Party, because of policy differences with other Congress leaders. He was the first Indian to become the Governor General of India.

His writings are characterised by a conversational ease which immediately develops a rapport with the reader. The present article is a part of the Convocation address that C. Rajgopalachari delivered at Madras University in 1948. The suggestions made by him in the address are relevant even today.

watch-word: slogan
artisan: skilled workman
amity: friendship
trite: not new
exertion: effort
denomination: name, designation
restraint: control

SCIENCE, HUMANITIES AND RELIGION

Sarvapalli Radhakrishnan (1888-1975) was primarily a teacher and a philosopher, though, after Independence, he occupied very high posts in the Government and acquitted himself with distinction. He was the Vice-President of India from 1952 to 1962 and President from 1962 to 1967. Dr Radhakrishnan authored many scholarly books, the more famous being *The Hindu View of Life* and *Indian Philosophy*. The present piece is the text, with a slight modification, of a speech he delivered at the Aligarh Muslim University.

jeopardy: peril

Blake: William Blake (1752-1827), English romantic poet, mystic, and visionary

Quranic: concerning the Koran, the sacred book of the Muslims

Masnavi: a Muslim philosopher

Sufi: Muslim mystic

I have become today one of them: He was made a member of the alumni and an honorary doctorate was conferred upon him.

WHAT IS CULTURE?

Jawaharlal Nehru (1889-1964), Prime Minister of India from 1947 to 1964, was one of the greatest leaders of the Indian people before and after Independence. A statesman of international repute, Nehru was also a master of pure, poetic English which throbs with passion and zest. His *Discovery of India* and *Autobiography* are works of enduring merit, and his speeches, published in several volumes, bear testimony to his love for freedom, world peace and international understanding.

aggressive: disposed to attack, offensive

dynamic: having force which produces change

pristine: ancient, good old

stagnation: becoming motionless, dull or sluggish

THE ETERNAL SILENCE OF THESE INFINITE CROWDS

Nirad Chaudhari (b. 1897) is one of the most controversial Indian writers in English. He gave up government service to edit *The Modern Review*, and then resigned his job as editor to become a free-lance journalist, The publication of his book *The Autobiography of an Unknown Indian* in 1951 shot him into fame. His other books *A Passage to England* and *The Continent of Circe* have been no less controversial. But the fact remains that he is a perceptive commentator on men and manners, and his language has a charm and grace of its own.

The piece presented here has been taken from *A Passage to England*

peck order: Pecking order; the social order among poultry in which any bird may peck a less important bird, but must submit being pecked by a more important or aggressive one.

gregarious: fond of the company of others.

adjacence: proximity; nearness

Agoras: places of assembly, especially market place.

Pascal: Bolaise Pascal (1623-1662), French philosopher and mathematician. The quotation is an adaptation of his sentence: "The eternal silence of these infinite spaces frightens me."

pub: tavern; a place where alchoholic beverages are served.

fended off: warded off; shut up

pariah: an untouchable

microcosm: a little universe or world

concubine: a woman who lives with a man although not legally married to him.

Comedie Humaine: the Human Comedy. This is the title given by Balzac to the entire corpus of his novels.

widest commonalty spread: from Wordsworth's line "joy in widest commonalty spread" in *The Excursion*.

NO MAN IS AN ISLAND
Minoo Masani

Minoo Masani (b. 1905) is a prolific writer on questions of public interest. He has written on subjects which concern only the Indian reality and also on topics which concern peoples of all nations. He is an optimist who believes that the present States would gradually merge into a World Union which would provide means to achieve a freer, fuller and richer life for each human being.

reconcile: bring into harmony

patent: government grant of exclusive privilege of making or selling a new invention

omniscience: infinite knowledge
despondent: without hope
reckon: calculate
dinosaur: a very large extinct reptile
brontosaurus: a large, prehistoric animal
straggler: a person who strays from the main path
surmount: overcome

THE BABUS OF NAYANJORE

Rabindranath Tagore (1861-1941) was a sage and reformer, writer and educator, patriot and internationalist all rolled in one. He wrote primarily in Bengali, but he himself translated many of his works into English. He was the first Indian to receive the Nobel Prize. He tried his hand at all forms of creative literature—poetry, drama, the novel and the short story—and excelled in all of them.

wiseacres: pretenders to learning

fomentation: application of warmth; bathing with warm or medicated lotions

foundered: filled with water and sank
repertory: stock
mirage: an optical illusion
paroxysm: convulsion

THE BROTHERS

Mulk Raj Anand (b. 1905) is one of the most widely known Indian novelists in English. He had his early education in Punjab, but later studied at the University of London and at Cambridge. His novels include *Coolie*, *Two Leaves and a Bud*. *The Sword and the Sickle*, *Untouchable*, *The Private Life of an Indian Prince* and *Morning Face*. Besides the novels Anand has also written a number of short stories dealing with Indian life and situations.

peremptory: impetuous, dictatorial

hardly any room to throw in a til seed: not enough space to accommodate even a grain of the size of gingili

circumspection: carefulness
torso: body
haven of escape: place to rest awhile
exorcie: appease, pacify
gaucheness: tactlessness
acha: all right
priggishly: in a mean, arrogant way
grimace of bonhommie: into a laughing gesture
barged in: broke in

AN ASTROLOGER'S DAY

R.K. Narayan (born 1906) ranks, with Raja Rao and Mulk Raj Anand, among the best Indian novelists writing in English. His novels and short stories, usually set in the fictitious town of

Malgudi, deal with the Indian way of life and the Indian character with great maturity and artistry. Among his novels are *Swami and Friends*, *The Bachelor of Arts*, *The Dark Room*, *The Financial Expert*, *Waiting for the Mahatma* and *The Guide*.

cowrie shells: shells of snails found in the Indian ocean
palmyra writing: writing on palm leaves
resplendent: bright
vociferous: noisy
impetuous nature: rash nature
jutka: a horse-drawn cart

COMPANIONS

Raja Rao (born 1909), one of the three greatest novelists of Indian English literature, was educated in Hyderabad, Aligarh and Paris, and now lives in the U.S.A. He has written four novels, *Kanthapura*, *The Serpent and the Rope* and *Cat and Shakespeare*, *Comrade Kirilov* and two collection of short stories, *The Cow of the Barricades* and *The Policeman and The Rose*. The present story has been taken from the second collection.

riposte: counterstroke; retort
quern: hand-mill for grinding corn
caravanserais: inns for caravans
minves. flirts
circumambulation: walking round
pall: cloth spread over a tomb

GLORY AT TWILIGHT

Bhavani Bhattacharya (born 1907) is one of the tallest figures in Indian English fiction. Some of his novels are *So Many Hungers*, *Music For Mohini*, *He who Rides a Tiger*, *A Goddess Named Gold*, *Shadow From Ladakh* and *A Dream in Hawaii*.

daughter-crisis: the liability of the father to get his daughter married
blind-man's staff: the only support
Ulu-ulu-ulu: ritualistic welcome sound made by women at a Bengali wedding

SPARROWS

Khwaja Ahmad Abbas(1914-1987) was a versatile genius whose activities ranged from journalism to film-making. But he was also a creative writer of distinction whose fictional works introduce the reader to a world of reality which is sometimes unbelievable. His two volumes of short stories, on which his reputation as a creative writer rests, are *Rice and Other Stories* and *One Thousand Nights on a Bed of Stone.*

fringed: adorned as a fringe or border
communal hookah: a hookah shared by all
patel: the headman of a village
obsequious: servile
charpoy: a common bedstead
banya: an Indian trader
furtive: secret
kafir: an unbeliever
docility: passive obedience
the badge of her tribe: the characteristic of the class of wives
second nature: acquired habit
ablutions: washing of the body or a part of it
vixen: a female fox

KARMA

Khuswant Singh (born 1915) has written a number of books on Sikh history and religion, and is one of the foremost journalists in English in India. He has two novels to his credit, *The Train to Pakistan* and *I Shall Not Hear the Nightingale*, and a collection of short stories, *The Mark of Vishnu and Other Stories.*

Saville Row: a fashionable row of tailors in London
aroma: fragrant smell
eau-de-cologne: perfume made in Cologne
Balliol: a famous college at Oxford
upteenth: several; many
koi hai?: Is there any one to take orders?
Ek chota: one small peg of whisky
zenana: the ladies' compartment
replenish: fill up again
obese: fat
coupe: two-seater saloon
haversacks: stout canvas bags for keeping things
Ek dam jao: get out at once
too much of the King's: too much of King's English.

THE FLOOD

Kamala Markandaya is one of the most important among the second generation of Indian novelists writing in English. She was born and brought up in south India and received her higher education in Madras University. But she now lives in London with her family. Her novels include *Nectar in a Sieve*, *Some Inner Fury*, *Silence of Desire*, *Possession*, *A Handful of Rice*, and *The Coffer Dams*. The present story, taken from Kamala Markandaya's first novel, is a story of quiet courage in the face of disaster.
vines : climbing plants
deflated : lacking in hope and energy
shack : a hut built of poor materials
tattoo : a series of beats
it claimed me : she fell asleep while she was sitting beside the flood

CIRCUS CAT, ALLEY CAT

Anita Desai (born 1937) is perhaps the most important among the women novelists in Indian English. Her novels include *Cry the Peacock*, *Foices in the City*, *Bye-bye, Blackbird*, *Where Shall We Go This Summer*, *Fire on the Mountain*, and *Clear Light of Day*. A number of her stories were included in the collection *Games at Twilight, and Other Stories.*

stucco house : a house covered with stucco, a mixture of cement, sand and lime

THE HOMECOMING

Arun Joshi (born 1939) is the author of four novels, *The Foreigner. The Strange Case of Billy Biswas*, *The Apprentice* and *The Labyrinth*. A few years back he received the Sahitya Academy Award for his works of fiction. He lives in Delhi and is in business.

the Eastern Front : The reference is to the Bangladesh Liberation War in 1971.

bazookas and mortars : different kinds of rocket launchers; cannons for throwing projectiles or aerial bombs

pincer and outflanking manoeuvre : names of various strategic movements of an army during a war